THE POEMS OF

JESUS

CHRIST

ALSO BY WILLIS BARNSTONE

Biblical

The Restored New Testament
The Other Bible: Jewish Pseudepigrapha, Christian Apocrypha,
Gnostic Scriptures, Kabbalah, Dead Sea Scrolls
The Apocalypse: The Book of Revelation
The New Covenant: Four Gospels and Apocalypse
The Gnostic Bible (with Marvin Meyer)
Essential Gnostic Scriptures (with Marvin Meyer)

Literary Criticism

Miguel de Cervantes's Rinconete y Cortadillo
The Poetics of Ecstasy: From Sappho to Borges
The Poetics of Translation: History, Theory, Practice
ABC of Translation

Poetry

Poems of Exchange
From This White Island
Antijournal
A Day in the Country
New Faces of China
China Poems
Overheard
A Snow Salmon Reached the Andes Lake
The Alphabet of Night

Ten Gospels and a Nightingale
Five A.M. in Beijing
Funny Ways of Staying Alive
The Secret Reader: 501 Sonnets
Algebra of Night: New and Selected Poems, 1948–1998
Life Watch
Café de l'Aube à Paris / Dawn Café in Paris
Stickball on 88th Street

Memoirs

Sunday Morning in Fascist Spain: A European Memoir, 1948–1953
With Borges on an Ordinary Evening in Buenos Aires
We Jews and Blacks: Memoir with Poems

Anthologies / Editions

Concrete Poetry: A World View (with Mary Ellen Solt)
Spanish Poetry, from Its Beginning through the Nineteenth Century
Modern European Poetry: French, German, Greek,
Italian, Russian, Spanish
Eighteen Texts: Writings by Contemporary Greek Authors
A Book of Women Poets from Antiquity to Now
(with Aliki Barnstone)
Literatures of Asia, Africa, and Latin America
(with Tony Barnstone)
Literatures of Latin America
Literatures of the Middle East (with Tony Barnstone)
Twenty-four Conversations with Borges, Including a Selection of Poems
(with Nicomedes Suárez Araúz)
Borges at Eighty: Conversations

Translations

THE POEMS OF
JESUS
CHRIST

TRANSLATED BY

Willis Barnstone

W. W. NORTON & COMPANY

NEW YORK · LONDON

All the poems in this volume are excerpted from Willis Barnstone,
The Restored New Testament, W. W. Norton, 2009. The source text for their translation from
Greek is the United Bible Societies *Greek New Testament*, 4th edition, 1993, from the 26th
edition of *Novum Testamentum Greaece*, edited by Eberhard and Erwin Nestle, based on an
earlier edition by Barbara and Kurt Aland (1979).

For information about permission to reproduce selections from this book,
write to Permissions, W. W. Norton & Company, Inc.,
500 Fifth Avenue, New York, NY 10110

For information about special discounts for bulk purchases, please contact
W. W. Norton Special Sales at specialsales@wwnorton.com or 800-233-4830

Manufacturing by Courier Westford
Book design by JAM Design
Production manager: Devon Zahn

Library of Congress Cataloging-in-Publication Data

Barnstone, Willis, 1927–
The poems of Jesus Christ / translated by Willis Barnstone. — 1st ed.
p. cm.
Includes bibliographical references (p.   ).
ISBN 978-0-393-08357-6 (hardcover)
1. Jesus Christ—Words. 2. Bible. N.T.—Language, style. I. Title.
BT306.B37 2012
226'.05209—dc23
2011047576

W. W. Norton & Company, Inc.
500 Fifth Avenue, New York, N.Y. 10110
www.wwnorton.com

W. W. Norton & Company Ltd.
Castle House, 75/76 Wells Street, London W1T 3QT

1 2 3 4 5 6 7 8 9 0

for my three children
Aliki Dora Barnstone
Robert Vassili Barnstone
Tony Dimitri Barnstone

CONTENTS

All the poems in this volume are excerpted from Willis Barnstone, *The Restored New Testament,* W. W. Norton, 2009. The source text for their translation from Greek is the United Bible Societies *Greek New Testament,* 4th edition, 1993, from the 26th edition of *Novum Testamentum Greaece,* edited by Eberhard and Erwin Nestle, based on an earlier edition by Barbara and Kurt Aland (1979).

JESUS CHRIST, THE INVISIBLE
POET IN THE GOSPELS

Jesus Christ is the great invisible poet of the world. Like the Old Testament prophets, he communicates in wisdom poetry—in short maxims, in narrative parable, and always in memorable metaphor. We hear the lyrical voice and his words are on our lips, yet implausibly for two millennia the lyricism has not been heard as poetry. What happened to blind us literarily to his wisdom poetry? In migrating from their Aramaic speech source into written Greek translation, and later into English translation, the lyrics got locked up in prose lineation. This shift of genre is strange since Jesus spoke uniformly in verse as did Hebrew Bible prophets. Indeed, the Bible begins with God speaking the universe into existence with the purest line of verse: "Let there be light!"[1] *The Poems of Jesus Christ* restores the poem to Jesus's voice. Consider his words in the gospels. In Mark Jesus is plain and powerful:

LOSING LIFE TO FIND THE SOUL

Those of you who would save your life
Will lose it.
Those of you who lose your life for me
And the good news

---

1 From the Hebrew יְהִי אוֹר (yehi or). Gen. 1.3.

Will save it.
How does it help a person to gain the whole world
And forfeit the soul?
What can a person give in exchange for the soul?

(Mk. 8.35–37)

In the Gospel of Matthew, the evangelist adds his own complexity and metaphors. Light signifies all things of mind, body, and earth:

LIGHT OF THE WORLD

You are the light of the world.
A city cannot be hidden when it is set on a mountain.
Nor do they light a lamp and place it below a basket,
    but on a stand,
And it glows on everyone in the house.
So let your light glow before people so they may see
    your good works
and your father of the heavens.

(Mt. 6.11–13)

Or meditate on Jesus's visionary "Birds of the Sky and Lilies of the Field." With its powerful imagery of temporality, "And if the grass of the field is there today / And tomorrow is cast into the oven," the poem seems to be a defiant forecast of the Holocaust:

Consider the lilies of the field, how they grow.
They do not labor or spin
But I tell you not even Shlomoh[2] in all his splendor

2 Solomon.

Was clothed like one of these lilies.
And if the grass of the field is there today
And tomorrow is cast into the oven
And in these ways God has dressed the earth,
Will he not clothe you in a more stunning raiment?

(Mt. 12.28–30)

And there is the unique anthem of the Bible:

THE LORD'S PRAYER

Our father who is in heaven,
Hallowed be your name.

Your kingdom come, your will be done
On earth as in heaven.

Give us today our daily bread
And forgive our debts

As we have forgiven our debtors.
And lead us not into temptation,

But rescue us from evil.

For yours is the kingdom,
And the power and glory forever.[3]

(Mt. 6.9–13)

3 This famous two-line ending of the Lord's Prayer is based on David's prayer in
1 Chronicles 29.11, but does not appear in the earliest Greek texts.

A few lines from Luke's "Sermon on the Plain" have the humane compassion and thrill of verses spoken by the Teacher in Ecclesiastes:

BLESSINGS SERMON ON THE PLAIN

Blessed are the poor
For yours is the kingdom of God.

Blessed are you who are hungry now
For you will be fed.

Blessed are you who weep now
For you will laugh.

(Lk. 6.20–21)

In Luke the brevity of a haunting maxim makes it enormous. Here Jesus urges his students to speak out:

I tell you, if you are silent,
The stones will weep.

(Lk. 19.14)

In John we hear a declaration of spiritual illumination in the child who will be the way to light:

For a little time longer the light is with you.
Walk about while you have the light
So that the darkness may not overtake you.
If you walk in the darkness
You do not know where you are going.
While you have light, believe in the light
So you may be the children of light.

(Jn. 12.35–36)

In the plainest speech John bespeaks spiritual despair, a plea, and a calm affirmation of mission:

NOW MY SOUL IS SHAKEN

Now my soul is shaken
And what shall I say?
Father, save me from this hour?
But I came for this hour.
Father, glorify your name.

(Jn. 12.27–28)

Given the constancy of his poetry, why has this universal misreading of Jesus's voice persisted into our days? The problem lies in translation. There is no original extant text in any form, poetic or prosaic, of Jesus's words. The gospel sources with his words remain unknown. We know that Jesus was not a Greek or a Roman but an Israeli Jew born in Galilee, who spoke his messianic words in his native Aramaic,[4] which by then was the spoken language of the Jews. His words appear in their earliest extant form translated from Aramaic into Greek in the Greek gospels of the New Testament composed some time between 75 C.E. and 100 C.E. From the Greek, the gospels were then translated into Syriac, Armenian, Coptic, Ethiopic, and Latin; many centuries later the gospels began to appear in all modern languages, including English.

In short we are not reading messianic Yeshua ben Yosef's own

---

4 Aramaic was the everyday language in Israel in the Second Temple period (539 B.C.E.–70 C.E.). While Jesus spoke Aramaic as his native language, when he attended synagogue he used Hebrew in his biblical readings, liturgy, and prayers. Ever since the Babylonian Captivity in the sixth century B.C.E., the Jews in Israel spoke Semitic Aramaic, although they used Hebrew in the temple.

voice in his own language of Aramaic. In their earliest preservation in the New Testament, we read a Greek translation from an unknown Aramaic source text, oral or written. For multiple reasons the original Aramaic verse that Jesus spoke as a wandering charismatic rabbi, teaching on the road and in the temples, came out in later translations as prose. Why? The translators did not understand the prosody of his Semitic poems, which is not as in Western literatures based on rhyme, meter, and stanzaic form, but on line parallelism and diverse sound patterns. The same veil of misunderstanding once lay over all the poetry of the Hebrew Bible from which a large part of Jesus's sayings derive. Then at the end of the nineteenth century, suddenly about half the Old Testament was rendered as verse, including most of Ecclesiastes, all of Job, the Proverbs, Song of Songs, Psalms, and most of the prophets. In all major translations since that critical discovery the Old Testament poetry has never slipped back into prose.

Today it would be unthinkable to translate the Book of Job as prose. Yet we must remember that the wondrous King James Version in 1611 translated even the inimitable lyrics of Solomon's "Song of Songs" from the Hebrew Bible as paragraphs of prose, turning the original Hebrew song into the "Prose of Prose." In reality Jesus's magnificent body of poetry was outwardly lost to the reader, though perhaps unconsciously perceived as verse because of its intense metaphoric impulse. The poetic images, the imaginative leaps, the wisdom paradoxes were all there, except for their lineation as verse. However, when the words of Jesus Christ set down as prose are read aloud—in churches usually chanted—in sound and persuasion they immediately return to poetry.

Just consider the last words uttered on the Roman cross, which is preserved in Hebrew: *Eli Eli lama sabachthani?* "My God, my God, why have you forsaken me?" The line in both Mark and Matthew repeats the immensely powerful line 1 of Psalm 21. The Book of Psalms, attributed to King David,[5] is a glory and arguably the most accomplished volume of poems ever composed. David is its singular poet. The poems of King David in the Old Testament have their counterpart in the poems of Jesus Christ in the New Testament. In *The Poems of Jesus Christ* the radiant poet is finally visible.

The voice of Jesus went through a thousand metamorphoses as it came to our times. In bringing about that transfer of sound and meaning, brave translators encountered many obstacles. There were always struggles. Yet in the course of his heretical, major translation of the New Testament into German at Wartburg Castle (1522), Martin Luther established the High German dialect as the national language of Germany.[6] The forty-seven scholars of the King James Version (1611) affected both spoken and written English deeply and poetically.

Some Bible translators lost their heads. The first translation of the complete New Testament into English was by John Wyclif in 1382. It appeared two years before his death. Wyclif was an Oxford don and master of Balliol College who believed that the common people should have access to scripture in English. He translated not from the Greek but through the additional linguistic veil of the Latin Vulgate, meaning his English version was at least three levels of translation away from Jesus's Aramaic speech: Aramaic > Greek > Latin > English. It was a superb version and became the most popular book in England, but he was soon declared a heretic. In 1415 his bones were dug up, burned, and thrown into the nearby river Swift.

William Tyndale did the first translation of the New Testament directly from the Greek into English rather than through the pre-

5 Scholars are uncertain of the actual date and authorship of the Psalms.
6 Luther's Bible did for German what Dante's *Divine Comedy* (1321) did for Italian and Chaucer's *Canterbury Tales* (1372) did for English in establishing a national language.

scribed Latin Vulgate. For his heretical act, the dissenting scholar was garroted and burnt at the stake. Citing Erasmus as his model, Tyndale proclaimed that his demotic version was for everyone, for "women, Scotts and Irishmen, Turks and Saracens . . . I would to God the plowman would sing a text at his plow and weaver at his loom to drive away the tediousness of time." His translation sang and revolutionized Bible translation. Celebrating ordinary Anglo-Saxon speech rather than Latin cognates, the Tyndale New Testament (1525) profoundly influenced English language and literature. Indeed about 80 percent of the King James Version comes directly from the Tyndale New Testament. Thereafter, the echo of Tyndale and the King James Version (1611) pervades the speech of Shakespeare, Milton, Blake, Dickinson, Whitman, Hopkins, Eliot, and Dylan Thomas. These poets have heard the song in the Bible and it infuses their work with a biblical lexicon deceptively modern.

With respect to poetry in the Bible, consider the following lines. Are they from Walt Whitman's "Song of the Broad Axe"?

> The carpenter measures with a line and makes an outline
>   with a marker;
> he roughs it out with chisels and marks it with compasses.
> He shapes it in the form of man, of man in all his glory, that
>   it may dwell in a shrine.
> He cut down cedars, or perhaps took a cypress or oak.
> He let it grow among the trees of the forest, or planted a
>   pine, and the rain made it grow.
> It is man's fuel for burning; some of it he takes and warms
>   himself, he kindles a fire and bakes bread.

This passage is not from Whitman but from Isaiah 44.12–15, a poet who wrote in the mid-sixth century B.C.E. But Whitman heard poetry concealed in prose in the Old Testament decades before it was common to set the lines as poetry. Western editors and translators did not detect the poetry (obvious to a native reader of Hebrew), since Hebrew lyric song, chanted psalm, and prophetic wisdom poems do not follow Greco-Roman and later European prosody of meter and rhyme. As noted Biblical Hebrew poetry is based on parallel units of verse and echoing sound patterns. Since the late nineteenth century, the leading editions of the Old Testament have set the poetical books in verse.

In 1966, for the first time, the New Testament of the Roman Catholic *Jerusalem Bible*[7] rendered all of Jesus's words as verse. Jesus's melodious wisdom poems find a poetic form in their redemptive version, which is courageous and often felicitous. With respect to poetic felicity in translation, quality inevitably depends on the aesthetic pen of both translator and original artist. Hence, two poets are at work: the original poet and the translating co-author. The abundantly annotated Jesuit translation of the Bible is a major scholarly achievement; but above all it liberates all words of Jesus from prose lineation, permitting them song as poetry in our English guesthouse. In the *Jerusalem Bible* the poet, no longer invisible, is Jesus.

Jesus is one among several outstanding poets in the New Testament who appear in the *Restored New Testament*. We have the Epistlers James and John whose letter poems are socially revolutionary with a deep compassion for the down and out and a disdain for the wealthy and powerful. The last book of the New Testament is attributed to John of Patmos, who in a cave on the Greek island of Patmos composed Revelation, the epic poem of the Bible. Revelation uses the metaphor of tyrannical Babylonia to disguise an incendiary attack on the oppressive Roman Empire and its "goat king"

7 The Jerusalem Bible (1966) is based on the original French version, *La bible de Jérusalem* (1956).

emperor, Caesar Augustus. Also known by the original Greek name "Apocalypse," Revelation's wild poetic images anticipate the great moments of blind King Lear standing on the mountain and raging into the cosmic heavens:

> When the lamb opened the sixth seal I looked
> And there took place a great earthquake
> And the sun became black like sackcloth of hair
> And the full moon became like blood,
> And the stars of the sky fell to the earth
> As the fig tree drops its unripe fruit
> Shaken by a great wind. And the sky
> Vanished like a scroll rolling up. . . .
>
> *(Rev. 6)*

Paul (Shaul by his Hebrew name) is the pioneer creator and missionary of the new Messianism (Christianity). Proudly calling himself "a Jew from the tribe of the Pharisees," he is unique for his passages on salvation through faith. Saint Paul is also an eloquent philosopher of being who masters complex thought with flawlessly easy rhetoric and poetic flare. His logical dexterity recalls the pre-Socratic Greek philosophers who also composed their speculations on existence in verse. Consider humanist Paul's sublime poetry in his discourse on love in 1 Corinthians:

> If I speak in the tongue of men and angels
> But have no love, I am but sounding brass
> Or a clanging cymbal. If I have prophecy
> And understand all mysteries and all knowledge
> And if I have all faith to remove mountains
> But love I do not have, then I am nothing.
> If I give all my goods to feed the poor

And give my body to be burned, and love
I do not have, in all I have gained nothing. . . .

When I was a child I spoke like a child,
I thought like a child and reasoned like a child.
When I became a man I put an end
To childish things. For now we look into
An enigmatic mirror. One day we will gaze
Face to face. Now I know in part, but then
I will know in full even as I am fully
Known. Now faith, hope, and love remain,
These three. Of these the greatest one is love.

(1 Cor. 13)

Matthew, like his model Mark, is a supreme storyteller. The scene is a village in Judea. His narrative genius is fulfilled in the poetic minimalism of Yeshua's precise order, as in a war zone, to prepare his final entry into Jerusalem. The moment is tense and dangerous. As in good poetry, there is no fluff. Each word counts. Yeshua says, laconically, in the passage here entitled "Entering Yerushalayim on a colt":

Go on into the village ahead of you
And soon you will find a donkey tethered
And her foal beside her.
Untie them and bring them to me.
And if anyone asks anything,
Say that their master needs them.
He will send them immediately.

(Mt. 21.2–3)

Then the voice changes as he addresses the daughter Israel (Jerusalem), telling her that her king is coming. In colorful irony, he moves with his royal retinue, which consists of himself, a donkey, and the donkey's foal. Providing hints of a terrible now and later salvation, he reveals that he, their king of the future, is about to ride humbly toward his fate as a prisoner who soon will die.

But for the moment, the role of the messiah is heady. Repeating and fulfilling the prophetic words of the Jewish prophet Zechariah, he is on the road. Cloaks have been placed on both his donkey and on the colt; and an enormous crowd—who have spread their cloaks and branches on the road—will walk before and after him, shouting as he rides:

RIDING ON A DONKEY

Say to the daughter Zion,
Who is Yerushalayim,
Look, your king is coming to you,
Humble and riding on a donkey
And on a colt,
The foal of a donkey.

(Mt. 21.5)

The passage spoken by Jesus cites Zechariah:

Rejoice greatly, O daughter Zion!
Shout aloud, O daughter Jerusalem!
Lo, your king comes to you:
triumphant and victorious is he,
humble and riding on a donkey,
on a colt, the foal of a donkey.

(Zech. 9.90)

As elsewhere, when verse passages from the original Hebrew Torah appear in the New Testament, in traditional renderings they are locked in prose. It is good to free them and let the music of their original song be overheard.

In the New Testament, Jesus is the unparalleled poet. His sayings, tales, and parables are plain, complex, and clear as open sky. Hence the universality of each lyric or narrative phrase he speaks. He speaks wisdom verse. The lines are imbued with joyful or sorrowful insight and inlight. Some are ancient one-line fragments, autonomous like a pulsating line by Sappho or Apollinaire. Others are long, such as "The Parable of the Lost Son." Seen together in the order they appear in each gospel, the poems operate as a parallel concise gospel story bequeathing the essence of the extended narration.

The sequences of spoken sage verse are gathered together here for the first time. They surprise as an unforeseen marvel, as perhaps the most significant and beautiful collection of wisdom poetry the world has known. With the Psalms of David they are the poetry galaxies of the Bible.

The poems are sometimes rich with garden, animal, and nature imagery; sometimes austere. They are never less than poignant as they move from diverse maxims to the culminating "darkness at noon" crucifixion and the sudden appearance of the resurrected messiah, wounded but walking and talking to his astonished students. In *The Poems of Jesus Christ* the drama is a solo performance. As the single actor, Jesus carries the totality of the tale in his cumulatively powerful voice. The poems from the Gospels of Mark, of Matthew, of Luke, of John, and of Thomas merge into one extraordinary naked verse drama: the Gospel of Jesus.[8]

---

8 In keeping with the notion of a single poetic drama, in moving from gospel to gospel where poems are virtually identical in word and theme, they are not repeated. However, if the same wisdom poem differs significantly, each version is repeated.

BON VOYAGE

After two millennia a Bible is a rainfall of languages. Jesus reads the Torah (Old Testament) in Hebrew, but his speaking tongue is Aramaic in which his name is likely to be Yeshua ben Yosef. In the gospels he is unexpectedly speaking to us in beautiful first-century demotic Greek. Then through the morning window of translation, he and his philosophical light and darkness enter this post-Babel book in English. We receive the story and his words with astonishment and do not question circumstance, which is just as well, for the story is a universe, whatever our origin or our faith or doubt. All ethno-religious epithets fade as clouds fade before the strong morning sun, and we enter the day and the night of the tale, never to return the same.

THE POEMS OF
JESUS
CHRIST

MARK
(Markos)

THE GOSPEL OF MARK is most often characterized as having been written by an author whose vernacular Greek is plain and rudimentary. Matthew, Luke, and John are more classical. But Mark is in many ways the greatest stylist among the evangelists. Commanding a minimal but compelling diction, he writes with clarity, concision, and dramatic power.

That Mark used the splendid, lively, demotic tongue of his time is genial. By using the spoken language of the people, he pioneered the speech of the New Testament. People could understand his "good news," his gospel. Had he chosen to compose the gospel in complex classical Greek, he would have had no popular audience. Similarly, daring Dante, Chaucer, and Montaigne also chose to write in vernacular Italian, English, and French, rather than in Latin, and thereby created the first great literatures in their homelands. The great Dutch humanist Erasmus praised gospel Greek for its universality, for being the tongue of "the plowboy of the fields."

Mark spoke to the laity, to the plowboy, the cobbler, and the carpenter. That flow of Mark's plain speech goes on today, even entering the work of Seamus Heaney, Ireland's Nobel laureate. In his recent *Human Chain*, Heaney retells the magical passage where Mark has described how the only way for Jesus to heal a paralytic in a house surrounded by crowds of followers is for the carpenters to uncover the roof and lower the paralytic man on his bed through the opening—an almost impossible task:

MIRACLE

Their shoulders numb, the ache and stoop deeplocked
In their backs, the stretcher handles
Slippery with sweat. And no let-up

Until he's strapped on tight, made tiltable
And raised to the tiled roof, then lowered for healing.
Be mindful of them as they stand and wait.[1]

Then in his own gospel verse—the source of Heaney's poem—
Jesus reveals clearly what is best to do for the man, solving any
dilemma of the heart:

DILEMMAS OF THE HEART

Why argue in your heart?

What is easier to say to the paralytic,
"Your wrongs are forgiven" or to say,
"Stand, pick up your bed, and walk"?

To know that the earthly son has the power
To forgive wrongs on earth,
I say, "Stand, pick up your bed, and go into your house."

(2.8–11)

1 Seamus Heaney, from "Miracle," *Human Chain* (New York: Farrar, Straus & Giroux, 2010), 16.

Mark's rhetoric is not of learned Cicero, Proust, and Henry James but rather of straightforward Mark Twain, Emily Dickinson, and Hemingway. The world is the common people of farm and village. In his dramatic metaphors of rich and poor; food and hunger; the leper seeking cure; the prostitute who loves; the farmer, plowboys, and carpenter, his Koine Greek is the perfect vehicle for the sonorous and precise beauty of Jesus's wisdom poetry.

COME FOLLOW ME

Come follow me
And I will make you fishers of people.

1.17

TO THE CONVULSING UNCLEAN SPIRIT IN A MAN

Be silent
And come out of him!

1.25

AT DAWN IN A DESOLATE PLACE

Let us go elsewhere into the neighboring towns
So I may preach there also. For this I came.

1.38

A LEPER ON HIS KNEES BEGS, "DO YOU WISH TO MAKE ME CLEAN?"

I wish to.
Now be clean.

1.41

DILEMMAS OF THE HEART

Why argue in your heart?

What is easier to say to the paralytic,
"Your wrongs are forgiven" or to say,
"Stand, pick up your bed, and walk"?

To know that the earthly son has the power
To forgive wrongs on earth,
I say, "Stand, pick up your bed, and go into your house."

2.8–11

WHO NEEDS A DOCTOR?

The strong have no need of a doctor,
But the sick do.
I came not to call on the just but on the stumblers.

2.17

THE BRIDEGROOM IS GONE

Can the attendants of the bridegroom fast
While the bridegroom is with them?

As long as the bridegroom is there,
They cannot fast. But days will come

When the bridegroom is seized by death.
On that day they will fast.

2.19–20

OLD CLOTH AND NEW WINE

No one sews an unshrunk patch of cloth
On an old garment

Since the new pulls the patch away from the old
And the tear becomes worse.

No one pours new wine in old skins,
Since the wine splits the skins

And both wine and skins are lost.
No, put new wine in a new skin.

2.21–22

THE HUNGRY ON SHABBAT[2]

Have you never read what David chose to do
When he was in need and hungry,

He and those with him?
How on the holy day of the High Priest Avyatar,

He went into the house of God and ate the loaves
Of consecrated bread that only priests are allowed to eat

And shared it with his companions?
The Shabbat was made for man and woman,

Not man and woman for Shabbat.
So the earthly son is rabbi even of the Shabbat.

2.25–28

PARABLE OF THE DIVIDED HOUSE

How can Satan cast out Satan?

If a kingdom is divided against itself
That kingdom cannot stand.

If a house is divided against itself
That house cannot stand.

2 The Sabbath.

And if Satan rises against himself and is divided
He cannot stand and collapses.

3.23–26

HOUSE OF THE STRONGMAN

No one can enter the house of the strongman
To plunder his possessions
Unless he first ties up the strongman.
Then he will plunder the house.

3.27

ASKING THE CROWD SITTING IN A CIRCLE, "WHO IS MY MOTHER?"

Who is my mother and who are my brothers?

Whoever does the will of my father in the skies
Is my brother and my sister and my mother.

3.33, 35

SOWER PARABLE

Look, the sower went out to sow
And it happened that as he sowed

Some seed fell on the road
And birds came and ate it.

Other seed fell on rocky ground
Where there was little soil,

And at once it sprang up
Because it lacked deep soil

And when the sun rose
It was scorched, and because

It had no roots it withered away.
Other seed fell among the thorns

And the thorns sprang up
And choked the sprouts

And it bore no grain,
But some fell into good soil

And it bore grain, growing
And increasing and it yielded

Thirty and sixty and one hundredfold.
Who has ears to hear, hear.

4.3–9

SECRET OF THE KINGDOM

You have been given the mystery of the kingdom of God.
For those outside, everything comes in parables
So they may look and not perceive,
So they may listen and not understand,
So they may not turn again and be forgiven.[3]

4.11–12

EXPLAINING THE SOWER PARABLE

The sower sows the word.
And these are the ones by the road
Where the word is sown.

When they hear it, at once Satan comes
And takes the word sown in them.
These are ones sown on rocky ground,

And when they hear the word
At once they receive it happily
And have no root in themselves

And endure only for a moment.
When trouble or persecution comes
Because of the word's sake,

At once they are shaky and fall.
Others are those sown among thorns.
These are ones who heard the word,

---

3 Final three lines are from Isaiah 6.9–10, whose meaning is a mystery.

But worldly cares and lure of wealth
And desires for other things come in
And choke the word and it turns barren.

And there are ones sown on good earth,
Who hear the word, receive it, and bear fruit
Thirty and sixty and one hundredfold.

4.14–20

LAMP ON A STAND

Is a lamp brought inside to be placed
Under a bushel basket or under the bed
And not set on a lampstand?
Nothing is hidden except to be disclosed
Or secret except to come into light.

4.21–22

MEASURE

Consider what you hear. The measure
You give will be the measure you get
And more will be given to you.
To those who have, more will be given,
And from those who have nothing
Even that nothing will be taken away.

4.24–25

SEED ON THE EARTH

The kingdom of God is like a man throwing seed
On the earth,

Sleeping and rising the night and day
To see the seed sprout and grow

In a way he cannot perceive.
On its own the earth bears fruit,

First grass, then a stalk, then the full grain in the ear.
But when the grain is ripe,

He immediately takes out his sickle.
The harvest has come.

4.26–29

PARABLE OF THE MUSTARD SEED AND THE KINGDOM OF GOD

To what can we compare the kingdom of God
Or in what parable shall we place it?
Like a mustard seed which is sown on the earth,
Smaller than all the seeds on the earth,
Yet when it is sown it grows and becomes greater
Than all the garden plants
And makes branches so big that under its shade
The birds of the sky may find there a place to nest.

4.30–32

SCOLDING THE WIND, HE SPEAKS TO THE SEA

Silence.
Be still.

4.39

WITH FEAR AND TREMBLING A WOMAN WITH TWELVE YEARS OF MENSTRUAL BLEEDING HAS TOUCHED HIS GARMENT

Who has touched my clothing?

Daughter, your faith has healed you.
Go in peace and be cured of your affliction.

5.30, 34

TO A SYNAGOGUE LEADER WHOSE DAUGHTER HAS DIED

Do not fear. Only believe.

Why this commotion and weeping?
The child did not die. No, she is sleeping.

Talitha koum.[4]
Girl, awake!

5.36, 39, 41

---

4 An Aramaic expression meaning, "Girl, awake!" Babylonian Aramaic was then the
language of Israeli Jews.

ON HEARING THAT HIS OWN SISTERS AND BROTHERS WERE OFFENDED

A prophet is not without honor
Except in his own country,
In his own family and in his own house.

6.4

GOING AROUND THE VILLAGES

Wherever you go into a house
Stay there until you leave.
And when a place will not receive or hear you,
As you leave, shake the dust off from under your feet
As a testimony against them.

6.10–11

ON JOINING HIS MESSENGERS

Come yourself alone to a deserted place
And rest a while.

6.31

His Students on a Ship in the Middle of a Stormy Sea Are Terrified When They See Him Walking Toward Them on the Waters

Take courage.
It is I.
Do not be afraid.

6.50

Child and Bread

Let the children be fed first.
It is not good to take the child's bread
And throw it to the dogs.

7.27

Compassion for the Crowd

I pity the crowd,
For they have been with me three days
And have nothing to eat.
If I send them hungry to their homes,
They will collapse on the road
And some have come from far away.

8.2–3

AFTER TAKING ONLY ONE LOAF OF BREAD ON THE SHIP, YESHUA DEFUSES AN ARGUMENT AMONG HIS STUDENTS

Why do you argue about not having bread?
Do you still not see or understand?
Has your heart hardened?

You have eyes, do you not see?
You have ears, do you not hear?

Don't you remember when I broke the five loaves
For the five thousand,
How many baskets filled with scraps you picked up?

Do you still not understand?

8.17–19, 21

FOLLOW ME

If some of you would follow me,
Deny yourself and take up your cross
And follow me.[5]

8.34

---

5 Authenticity uncertain. Although Jesus foresees his death (Mk. 9.31, 10.32), the crucifixion has not yet occurred and the cross is not yet a symbol of Christian devotion.

LOSING LIFE TO FIND THE SOUL

Those of you who would save your life
Will lose it.
Those of you who lose your life for me
And the good news
Will save it.
How does it help a person to gain the whole world
And forfeit the soul?
What can a person give in exchange for the soul?

8.35–37

TASTING DEATH

There are some of you standing here
Who will not taste death
Until you see that the kingdom of God has come
With all its power.

9.1

I WILL DIE AND BE ARISEN

The earthly son will be handed over into human hands
And they will kill him,
And three days after being killed he will arise.

9.31

CHILD IN HIS ARMS

Whoever welcomes a child
In my name also welcomes me

And whoever welcomes me welcomes
The one who sent me.

9.37

A MILLSTONE AROUND YOUR NECK AND
THROWN IN THE SEA

If you have made a young believer stumble,
It is better to hang a millstone around your neck
And be thrown into the sea.

If your hand makes you stumble, cut it off.
It is better to enter life maimed than to have two hands
And descend into the unquenchable fires of hell,[6]

If your foot makes you stumble, cut it off.
It is better to enter life maimed than to have two feet
And descend into hell.

If your eye makes you stumble, tear it out.
It is better to enter one-eyed into the kingdom of God
Than to have two eyes

6 Hell, a pit of darkness. In Hebrew Gei Hinnom, meaning the Valley of Hinnom.

And be flung into hell where the worm does not die
And the fire lives unextinguished.

9.42–48

Salted with Fire

Everyone will be salted with fire.
Salt is good, but if salt loses the taste of salt,
What will you season with?
Keep the salt in yourselves and be at peace
With one another.

9.49–50

Divorce of Man and Woman

From the beginning of creation
God made us male and female.
Because of that a person will leave the father and mother
And the two will be one flesh.
They are no longer two but one flesh.
So what God joined together let no one separate.

10.6–9

Let the Children Come to Me

Let the children come to me.
Do not stop them. For the kingdom of God
Belongs to them.

I tell you,
Whoever does not receive the kingdom of God
Like a child
Will never enter therein.

10.14–15

THE RICH MAN

One thing you lack. Go and sell all you own
And give it to the poor
And you will have a treasure in heaven.
Then come and follow me.

10.21

HEAVEN THROUGH THE EYE OF A NEEDLE

How hard it will be for those with money
To enter the kingdom of God!
Children, how hard it is to enter the kingdom of God.
It is easier for a camel to go through the eye of a needle
Than for a rich man to enter the kingdom of God.[7]

10.23–25

7 In converting an Aramaic proverb into Greek, through a misreading of the consonants a "coarse thread" became a "camel," fortuitously creating a wondrous metaphor. See note 108 in the *Restored New Testament*.

THE FIRST WILL BE LAST

There is no one who gives up home or brothers or sisters
Or mother or father or children or farms

For my sake and for the good news,
Who will not receive a hundredfold.

In this age you suffer persecutions, losing houses
And brothers and sisters and mothers

And children and farms
Yet in the age to come you will gain life everlasting.

Many who now are first will be last
And the last will be first.

10.29–31

I WILL DIE AND BE ARISEN

We are going up to Yerushalayim
And the earthly son will be handed over to the high priests
And the scholars,
And they will condemn him to death
And hand him over to the Romans
And they will ridicule him and spit on him and flog him
And kill him
And after three days he will rise again.

10.33–34

To Be First Be a Slave

Among the Romans, those who are called the rulers
Lord over the people and their great ones wield power.
You know that. But it's not so with you.
Whoever would be great among you must become your
    slave.
Whoever would be first must be the slave of all.
The earthly son did not come to be served
But to serve and give his life as ransom for the many.

10.42–45

To a Blind Beggar in Yeriho,[8] Crying, "Rabboni,[9] Have Pity on Me! Let Me See Again"

Go, your faith has cured you.

10.52

Untamed Colt on the Road to Jerusalem

Go into the village before you
And once you are inside you will find a tethered colt
On which no one has sat.
Untie it and bring it.
If someone tells you, "Why are you doing this?" say,
His master needs it and he will send it back at once.

11.2–3

8 Jericho.
9 *Rabboni* in Aramaic means "my great rabbi."

MOVING MOUNTAINS

If you tell this mountain, "Rise and leap into the sea,"
And have no doubt in your heart

But believe that what is said will happen,
It will be yours.

So I say to you,
All that you pray and ask for, believe that you have received it

And it will be yours.
When you stand praying, if you hold something

Against someone, forgive
So your father will also forgive your wrong steps.

11.23–25

PARABLE OF THE UNBRIDLED TENANTS

A man planted a vineyard and put a fence
Around it, dug a wine vat and built a tower.

He rented it to farmers and left the country.
At the harvest he sent a slave to the farmers

To take back some fruits from the vineyard.
But they seized him, lashed him, and sent him away

Empty. Again he sent another slave to them
And him they struck on the head and insulted.

He sent another and that one they killed,
And many more, lashing some, killing others.

He still had one beloved son. He sent him
Finally to them, saying, "They will respect

My son." But those farmers said to one another,
"This is the heir. Come, let us kill him

And the inheritance is ours." They seized him
And killed him and threw him outside the vineyard.

What will the owner of the vineyard do?
He will come and destroy the farmers and give

The vineyard to others. Have you not read
In the Psalms: "A stone that the builders rejected

Became the cornerstone. From the Lord
It came to be and is wonderful in our eyes."

12.1–11

To Rome and to God

The things of Caesar give to Caesar
And the things of God give to God.

12.17

THE PRIMARY COMMANDMENTS

"Hear O Yisrael, the lord our God, the lord is one.

You will love the lord our God with all your heart
And all your soul and all your mind and all your might."

"You will love your neighbor like yourself."[10]

12.29–31

WATCH OUT FOR THE SCHOLAR

Beware of the scholars, the ones in long robes
Who love to stroll about, be greeted in the marketplace
And claim the best seats in the synagogue
And the foremost couches at dinner,
Who eat up the widow's house
And solely for show say long prayers.
They will receive the greater condemnation.

12.38–40

THE WIDOW'S COPPER COINS

That poor widow threw in more than all who cast money
Into the treasury.
They have all thrown in from their abundance.

10 Exod. 3.6 and 3.15.

She has thrown in from her poverty.
She gave all that she had to live on.

12.43–44

ON THE MOUNTAIN OF OLIVES WITH HIS FOUR STUDENTS, YESHUA PROPHESIES DESTRUCTION

Beware that no one leads you astray.
Many will come in my name saying, "I am,"

And they will lead many astray.
But when you hear of wars and rumors of wars

Do not be frightened. These things must occur.
But the end is not yet.

Nation will rise against nation, kingdom against kingdom,
There will be earthquakes in the lands

And there will be famines.
These things are the beginnings of the last agonies.

13.5–8

YOU WILL BE HATED BECAUSE OF ME BUT SURVIVE

Look out for yourselves. They will hand you over
To the Sanhedrin and lash you in the synagogues
And you will stand before governors and kings

Because of me and testify to them. And first
You must preach the good news to all peoples.
When they turn you over and bring you to trial,

Don't worry beforehand about what you will say.
Whatever is given to you in that hour, say it,
For it is not you who speak but the holy spirit.

Then brother will hand over brother to death
And father his child, and children will rise up
Against parents and put them to death.

And you will be hated by everyone
Because of my name. But whoever survives
To the end, that person will be saved.

13.9–13

DESOLATION IN YEHUDA[11]

When you see the "abomination of desolation"
Standing where it should not—let the reader
Understand—then let those in Yehuda flee
To the mountains, and someone on the rooftop

Not come down or go into the house
To take things away, and a man in the fields
Not go back to pick up clothing left behind.

11 Judea or Israel.

Grief to women with a child in the womb
And to women nursing babies in those days!
Pray that it may not happen in the winter.

In those days there will be an affliction
Which has not happened since the beginning
Of creation, which God created, until now,
And no, in no way again will take place.

And if the Lord had not shortened the days,
No flesh would be saved. But for the one
Whom he chose, he did shorten the days.

13.14–20

THE EARTHLY SON COMES IN THE CLOUDS

And then, if someone says to you, "Look,
Here is the messiah, look, he is there,"
Do not believe. False messiahs and false prophets[12]
Will rise up and perform signs and wonders

To mislead the chosen, if they can.
But beware! I have forewarned all to you.
But in those days after that affliction,
The sun will be darkened

---

12 These "false messiahs" and "false prophets" are not Jesus's coreligionist Jews but the Gnostics, those who come with knowledge rather than faith, and they were Gnostic Jews, Gnostic Christians, and Gnostic pagans. The Gnostics were the main ideological enemies during the later period of church formation. As such, these warnings reflect not specific concerns in Jesus's lifetime but fierce sectarian rivalries in the period of the later evangelists.

And the moon not give its light
And the stars will fall out of the sky
And the powers in heaven will quake.
Then you will see the earthly son coming

On clouds with great power and glory.
Then he will send out angels and gather in
The chosen from the four winds from the end
Of the earth to the deep end of the sky.

13.21–27

STAY AWAKE FOR THE COMING

From the fig tree learn the parable.
When its branch is tender again and shoots out leaves,
You know that summer is near.

So when you see these things happening
You know that the earthly son is near the doors.
This generation will not pass away before

All these things have come about.
The sky and the earth will pass away
But my words will not pass away.

But of that day or the hour no one knows,
Neither the angels in heaven nor the son.
Only the father. Be watchful, stay awake.

You do not know when the time will come.
It is like when a person goes on a journey
And puts slaves in charge, to each his task,

And commands the doorkeeper to be watchful.
Be watchful then, you never know when the lord
Of the house comes, in the evening or midnight

Or at cockcrow or dawn, or coming suddenly
He may find you asleep.
What I say to you I say to everyone. Beware.

13.28–37

ANOINTED BY A WOMAN IN THE HOUSE OF THE LEPER

Let her be. Why do you bother her?
She has done a good thing for me.
You always have the poor with you
And whenever you want you can do good for them.
But me you do not always have.
She did what she could.
She prepared ahead of time to anoint my body for the burial.
Wherever in the whole world the good news is preached,
What this woman did will speak her memory.

14.6–9

PLANNING THE SEDER[13] IN THE UPPER ROOM

Go into the city and you will meet
A man carrying a clay pot of water.
Follow him and wherever he enters tell
The owner of the house, "The rabbi asks,
'Where is my guest room where I may eat
The Pesach supper with my students?'
And he will show you a large upper room
Furnished and ready. There prepare for us."

14.13–15

RECLINING FOR THE SEDER SUPPER WITH THE TWELVE, HE PROPHESIES

One of you will betray me,
One who is eating with me, one of the twelve
Who is dipping the matzot bread[14] in the bowl.

The earthly son will leave,
But a plague on him who betrayed the earthly son!
It would be better for him had he not been born!

14.18, 20–21

13 The Last Supper.
14 The unleavened bread that Jesus breaks at the Seder ceremony is in Hebrew *matzot(h)*. The Seder celebrates the Passover, the Pesach supper, when the Jews fleeing their captivity in Egypt had time to bake only unleavened bread.

BREAKING THE BREAD AND POURING THE WINE

Take it. This is my body.
This is my blood of the covenant
Poured out for the many.
Amain, I say to you.
I will no longer drink the fruit of the vine
Until the day I drink it new in the kingdom of God.

14.22, 24–25

YOU WILL ALL FAIL ME

You will all stumble and fail me.
"I will strike down the shepherd
And the sheep will be scattered."[15]
But after I am raised up I will lead the way
For you into the Galil.

14.27–28

BEFORE THE COCK CROWS TWICE
(answering Simon Peter who says he will never fail him)

Today on this same night before the cock crows twice
You will deny me three times,

[Shimon]   Even if I must die for you, I will not deny you.

14.31

---

15 Jesus is quoting the prophet Zechariah.

TERROR AND PRAYER ON THE MOUNTAIN OF OLIVES

Sit here while I pray.
My soul is in sorrow to the point of death.
Stay here and keep awake.

14.32, 34

ABBA, MY FATHER, TAKE THIS CUP FROM ME

Abba,[16] my father, for you all things are possible.
Take this cup from me.
Not what I will but what you will.

14.36

CATCHING SHIMON KEFA ASLEEP

Shimon, are you sleeping? Did you not have
The strength to keep awake for an hour?
Stay awake and pray that you are not tested.
Oh, the spirit is ready but the flesh is weak.

14.37–38

16 Abba is Aramaic for "Father."

WAKE, FOR BETRAYAL IS NEAR

Sleep what is left of the night and rest.
Enough! The hour has come.
Look, the earthly son is betrayed
Into the hands of those who do wrong.
Get up and let us go.
Look, my betrayer is drawing near.

14.41–42

TO A CROWD WITH SWORDS AND CLUBS

As against a thief have you come with swords
And clubs to arrest me?
I was with you every day in the Temple, teaching,
And you did not seize me,
Only now you act
So the scriptures may be fulfilled.

14.48–49

THE PRIEST ASKS, "ARE YOU THE MESSIAH, THE SON OF THE BLESSED ONE?"

I am.

14.62

YESHUA RESPONDS TO THE PRIEST, CITING DANIEL AND PSALMS

"And you will see the earthly son seated on the right
  of the power
And coming with the clouds of heaven."[17]

14.62

PILATUS ASKS HIM, "ARE YOU THE KING OF THE JEWS?"

You say it.

15.2

DARKNESS AT NOON

Eloi Eloi, lema sabachtani?
My God, my God, why do you abandon me?[18]

15.34

17 Cited from Daniel 7.13 and Psalms 110.1.
18 Jesus's words are in Aramaic, from Psalm 22, line 1. In Matthew the same phrase is cited in Hebrew.

The Supplement of Mark[19]

YESHUA APPEARS FIRST TO MIRYAM OF MAGDALA AND THEN TO THE ELEVEN DISBELIEVING STUDENTS RECLINING AT THE TABLE

Go into all the world and proclaim the good news to all
    creation.
Who believes and is immersed will be saved
And who is unbelieving will be condemned.
And signs will accompany the believers.
In my name they will cast out demons
And speak in new tongues.
They will pick up serpents with their hands,
They will drink poison; it will not harm them.
They will lay their hands on the sick who will be well again.

16.15–19

19 "The Longer Ending of Mark" is an "orphan ending," meaning that it is likely to be an emendation added in the mid- to late second century. The UBS *Fourth Corrected Edition* of the Greek texts brackets the ending as "doubtful." It adds motifs with no parallel in the New Testament, such as the "snakes and drinking poison." The pathos of the crucifixion scene in Mark yields to later evangelizing exhortation reflecting an already established church. This ending may have been added to make Mark conform to the resurrection passages that do appear in Matthew and Luke. John also has no original resurrection scene, and like Mark has a supplemental ending of later origin.

MATTHEW
(Mattityahu)

THE GOSPEL OF MATTHEW may be said to be the most apho-
ristic and poetic of the gospels and closest to a sayings book. It
is largely poetry. This teaching book does not have the same austere
plainness and drama of Mark, which is more uniformly narrative
and ends abruptly at a moment of fear and ecstasy in the cave where
Jesus's body has disappeared. But Matthew also has pathos and con-
veys a sense of Jesus as a leader of the poor, of the disenfranchised,
in an epic of hunger and hope.

Matthew uniquely covers many aspects of the life and mission of
Jesus, including the coming of the Magi and Jesus's birth and circumcision. His extraordinary poetic and philosophical contribution
is his gathering of the great sequence of poems, which is the Sermon on the Mount, comprising the Beatitudes and the Lord's
Prayer. His "Birds of the Sky and Lilies of the Field" is profound
and exquisitely beautiful. Along with Revelation, the epic poem of
the New Testament, the poetry in Matthew takes its place among
the great bodies of world poetry.

TEMPTATION IN THE DESERT

One lives not on bread alone
But on every word coming through the mouth of God.

4.4

FOR THOSE SITTING IN THE LAND AND SHADOW OF DEATH

Land of Zvulun and land of Naftali,
The way to the sea beyond the Yarden,
The Galil of the foreigners,
The people who were sitting in darkness
Saw a great light,
And for those sitting in the land and shadow of death
The light sprang into dawn.

4.15–16

WITH FISHERMEN CASTING THEIR NETS INTO THE SEA OF THE GALIL

Come, and I will make you fishers of people.

4.19

SERMON ON THE MOUNTAIN[1]

Blessed are the poor in spirit
For theirs is the kingdom of heaven.

Blessed are they who mourn
For they will be comforted.

Blessed are the gentle
For they will inherit the earth.

Blessed are the hungry and thirsty for justice
For they will be heartily fed.

Blessed are the merciful
For they will obtain mercy.

Blessed are the clean in heart
For they will see God.

Blessed are the peacemakers
For they will be called the children of God.

Blessed are they who are persecuted for the sake of justice,
For theirs is the kingdom of heaven.

---

1 Chapters 5–7, 10, 13, 18, 24–25 are commonly known as the Sermon on the Mount, a phrase that does not appear in the New Testament. The Sermon is a compilation of wisdom sayings of Yeshua and contains the Beatitudes (blessings) (5.3–12). Parts of the Sermon are found dispersed in the other gospels, and have a counterpart in Luke's Sermon on the Plain (Luke 6.20–49).

Blessed are you when they revile, persecute, and speak
Every cunning evil against you and lie because of me.

Rejoice and be glad, for your reward in the heavens is huge,
And in this way did they persecute the prophets before you.

5.3–12

SALT

You are the salt of the earth.
But if the salt has lost its taste, how will it recover its salt?
Its powers are for nothing except to be thrown away
And trampled underfoot by others.

5.13

LIGHT OF THE WORLD

You are the light of the world.
A city cannot be hidden when it is set on a mountain.
Nor do they light a lamp and place it below a basket,
But on a stand,
And it glows on everyone in the house.
So let your light glow before people so they may see
Your good works
And glorify your father of the heavens.

5.14–16

FULFILLING THE WORDS OF THE PROPHETS

Do not think that I have come to destroy the law or the
    prophets.
I have not come to destroy but to fulfill.
And yes I say to you, until the sky and the earth are gone,
Not one tiny iota or serif will disappear from the law
Until all has been completed.
Whoever breaks even the lightest of the commandments
And teaches others to do the same
Will be esteemed least in the kingdom of heaven,[2]
But whoever performs and teaches them
Will be called great in the kingdom of heaven.
I say to you, if you don't exceed the justice
Of the scholars and the Prushim,[3]
You will never enter the kingdom of heaven.

5.17–20

BE RECONCILED WITH YOUR COMPANION

You have heard our people say to those in ancient times,[4]
    You must not murder,
    And whoever murders will be liable to judgment.
I say to you, whoever is angry with a companion
Will be judged in court,
And whoever calls a companion a fool will go before
The Sanhedrin, the highest court,

2 Literally, "the kingdom of the skies."
3 Pharisees.
4 Exod. 20.13.

And whoever calls a companion a scoundrel
Will taste the fire of Gei Hinnom.[5]
If then you bring your gift to the altar,
And there you remember your companion holds something
    against you,
Leave your gift before the altar,
And go first to be reconciled with your companion
And then come back and present your offering.

                                                    5.21–24

TURN YOUR CHEEK

And you have heard it said,
"An eye for an eye and a tooth for a tooth."[6]
But I tell you not to resist the wicked person,
And if someone strikes you on the right cheek,
Turn your other cheek as well.
If someone wants to sue you for your shirt,
Give him your cloak as well.
If someone forces you to go a mile with him,
Go a second mile with him.
Give to who asks you. And do not turn away one
Who wants to borrow from you.

                                                    5.38–42

5 Gehenna from the Hebrew Gei Hinnom, meaning the "Valley of Hinnom." *Gei
Hinnom* and *Sheol* are normally translated as "hell," though biblical hell was simply a
burial place, with no punishment.
6 Exod. 21.23–24.

LOVE YOUR ENEMIES

You have heard it said,
"You will love your neighbor and hate your enemy."[7]
I say to you to love your enemies
And pray for those who persecute you
So you may become the children of your father in heaven,
For he makes the sun rise over the evil and the good,
And he brings the rains to the just and the unjust among us.
If you love those who love you, what reward have you?
Do not even the tax collectors do the same?
If you greet only those who are your friends,
How have you done more than others?
Have you done more than the gentiles?
Be perfect as your father the heavenly one is perfect.

5.43–48

ACTORS IN THE SYNAGOGUE

Take care not to perform your good deeds before other
   people
So as to be seen by them,
For you will have no reward from your father in heaven.
When you give alms, don't sound a ram's horn before you
Like the actors in the synagogues and in the streets,
Who seek the praise of the onlookers.
I say to you, they have their reward.
Yet when you give alms, do not let the left hand know

7 Lev. 19.18.

What the right hand is doing
So the alms may be given in secret,
And your father seeing you in secret will repay you.

6.1–4

THE LORD'S PRAYER

Our father who is in heaven,
Hallowed be your name.

Your kingdom come, your will be done
On earth as in heaven.

Give us today our daily bread
And forgive our debts

As we have forgiven our debtors.
And lead us not into temptation,

But rescue us from evil.[8]

[For yours is the kingdom,
And the power and glory forever.][9]

6.9–13

8 The figure referred to is probably the devil.
9 This famous ending of the Lord's Prayer is in brackets, since this doxology, based on David's prayer in 1 Chronicles 29.11, does not appear in the earliest Greek texts.

FORGIVING

If you forgive those who have stumbled and gone astray
Then your heavenly father will forgive you,
But if you will not forgive others
Your father will not forgive your missteps.

6.14–15

TREASURES IN HEAVEN

Do not hoard your treasures on earth
Where moth and earthworms consume them,
Where thieves dig through walls and steal them,
But store your treasures in heaven
Where neither moth nor earthworm consumes
And where thieves do not dig through the walls and steal,
Your treasure is also there where your heart will be.

6.19–21

LAMP OF THE BODY

The lamp of the body is the eye.
If your eye is clear, your whole body is filled with light,
But if your eye is clouded, your whole body
Will inhabit darkness.
And if the light in your whole body is darkness,
How dark it is!

6.22–23

DILEMMA OF TWO MASTERS

No one can serve two masters.
You will either hate one and love the other
Or cling to one and despise the other.
You cannot serve God and the mammon[10] of riches.

6.24

LIFE IS MORE THAN FOOD

So I tell you, do not worry about your life
Or say, "What am I to eat? What am I to drink?"
And about the body, "What am I to wear?"
Is life not more than food,
Your body not more than clothing?

6.25

BIRDS OF THE SKY AND LILIES OF THE FIELD

Consider the birds of the sky.
They do not sow or reap or collect for their granaries,
Yet your heavenly father feeds them.
Are you not more valuable than they?
Who among you by brooding can add one more hour
To your life?

And why care about clothing?
Consider the lilies of the field, how they grow.

10 One fond of money.

They do not labor or spin
But I tell you not even Shlomoh[11] in all his splendor
Was clothed like one of these lilies.
And if the grass of the field is there today
And tomorrow is cast into the oven
And in these ways God has dressed the earth,
Will he not clothe you in a more stunning raiment,
You who suffer from poor faith?

6.26–30

BROODING ABOUT TOMORROW

Do not worry about tomorrow,
For tomorrow will worry about itself.
Each day has enough troubles of its own.

6.34

SPLINTER IN THE EYE

Do not judge so you may not be judged,
For by your judgment you will be judged
And by your measure you will be measured.

Why do you gaze at the splinter in your brother's eye
Yet not recognize the log in your own eye?
Why say to your brother,

---

11 Solomon.

"Let me take the splinter out of your eye"
When your own eye carries a log of wood?

Hypocrite. Remove the log from your own vision,
And you will see clearly enough
To pluck the sliver from your brother's eye.

7.1–5

PEARLS AND PIGS

Do not give the holy to the dogs
Or cast your pearls before the pigs.
They will probably trample them underfoot
And turn and tear you to pieces.

7.6

KNOCK AND THE DOOR WILL BE OPENED

Ask and it will be given to you.
Seek and you will find.
Knock and the door will be opened for you.
Everyone who asks receives
And the seeker finds,
And the door will be opened to one who knocks.
And who among you if your son asks for bread
Will give him stone?
Or if he asks for fish will give him a snake?
If you, who are nimble-minded, know how to give good gifts

To your children,
How much more will your father of the skies
Give good gifts to those who ask him?

7.7–11

DOING FOR OTHERS

Whatever you wish others to do for you,
So do for them.
Such is the meaning of the law and the prophets.

7.12

NARROW GATE

Go in through the narrow gate,
Since wide is the gate and spacious the road
That leads to destruction,
And there are many who go in through it.
But how narrow is the gate and cramped is the road
That leads to life,
And there are few who find it.

7.13–14

WOLVES IN SHEEP'S CLOTHING

Beware of false prophets
Who come to you in sheep's clothing,
But who inwardly are wolves.[12]

7.15

TREE AND FRUIT

From their fruit you will know them.
Can you gather grapes from thorns or pick figs from thistles?
Every good tree bears delicious fruit,
But the diseased tree bears rotting fruit.
A good tree cannot yield rotting fruit,
Nor a diseased tree delicious fruits.
Every tree incapable of delicious fruit is cut down
And tossed in the fire.
So from their fruit you will know them.

7.16–20

WIND BATTERING HOUSES

Everyone who hears my words and follows them
Will be like the prudent man who built his house upon the
   rock.
The rain fell and the rivers formed

---

12 The phrase "false prophets" probably refers to the Gnostics.

And the winds blew and battered that house
And it did not fall down
Because it was founded upon the rock.

But everyone who hears my words and doesn't follow them
Will be like the foolish man who built his house upon the
    sand.
The rain fell and the rivers formed
And the winds blew and battered that house
And it fell down and it was a great fall.

7.24–27

No Place to Rest

Foxes have holes in the earth
And birds of the sky have nests,
But the earthly son has no place to rest his head.

8.20

Follow Me

Follow me
And let the dead bury their own dead.

8.22

UNSHRUNK CLOTH AND NEW WINE

No one sews a patch of unshrunk cloth on an old coat,
Since the patch pulls away from the coat
And makes the tear worse.
Nor do they pour new wine into old wineskins.
If they do, the skins burst, the wine gushes out,
And the wineskins are ruined.
No, they pour new wine into fresh wineskins
And both are preserved.

9.16–17

INSTRUCTIONS TO HIS TWELVE STUDENTS

Don't go on the road where there are gentiles
And don't enter the city of the Shomroni.[13]
Go rather to the lost sheep of the house of Yisrael.
And as you go, preach,
And that the kingdom of heaven is coming near.
Heal the sick, raise the dead, cleanse the lepers,
And cast out the demons.
As you have freely received, freely give.
Don't take gold and silver and copper in your belts,
Or a bag for the journey
Or two tunics or sandals or a staff,
For the laborer earns his food.

10.5–10

13 Samaritans.

SHAKE THE DUST FROM YOUR FEET

In whatever city or village you enter,
Find out who in it is worthy
And stay there until you leave.
As you go into a house, greet it,
And if the house is worthy
Let your peace be upon it.
But if the house is not worthy,
Let your peace return to you.
If someone doesn't welcome you
Or listen to your words,
As you go out of that house or city
Shake the dust from your feet.
Amain, I say to you,
Sedom and Amorah[14] will be more tolerable
On the day of judgment
Than the fate of that city.

10.11–15

BE CRAFTY AS SNAKES, INNOCENT AS DOVES

Look, I send you out as sheep among wolves,
So be crafty as snakes and innocent as doves.
Be careful of people who will hand you over to the councils
And flog you in their synagogues.
You will be dragged before governors and kings,
Because of me, to bear witness before them
And before the gentiles.

---

14 Sodom and Gomorrah.

But when they hand you over,
Do not worry about how and what you are to say.
In that hour what you say will be given to you,
For you will not be speaking.
The spirit of your father will be speaking through you.

Brother will hand brother over to death,
And a father will turn in his child,
And children will rise against their parents
And have them put to death.
You will be hated by all because of my name,
But the one who endures to the end will be saved.
And when they persecute you in one city,
Escape to another.
You will not have gone through the cities of Yisrael
Before the coming of the earthly son.

10.16–23

STUDENT TO TEACHER, SLAVE TO MASTER

A student is not above the teacher
Or a slave above the master.
It is enough for the student to be like the teacher
And the slave like the master.
If they call the master of the house Baal Zebul,[15]
Lord of the flies,
How much worse will they call the members
Of the household!

10.24–25

15 Beelzebul.

UNCOVERING DARKNESS

So do not fear them.
There is nothing concealed that will not be revealed
And nothing hidden that will not be known.
What I say to you in darkness, speak in the light,
And what you hear whispered in your ear,
Proclaim from the housetops.
And have no fear of those who kill the body
But are unable to kill the soul.
Fear rather the one who destroys
Both soul and body in Gei Hinnom.

10.26–28

TWO SPARROWS AND A PENNY

Are two sparrows not sold for a penny?
Yet not one of them will fall to the earth
Apart from your father,
Even the hairs of your head are each counted.
So have no fear.
You are worth more than many sparrows.

10.29–31

Not Peace but a Sword

Do not think I have come to bring peace on the earth.
I have not come to bring peace but a sword.
I came to set a man against his father
And a daughter against her mother,
And a bride against her mother-in-law
And one's enemies will be in one's household.

10.34–36

Finding Soul

If you love your father or mother more than me,
You are not worthy of me,
If you love your son or daughter more than me,
You are not worthy of me,
And if you do not take up the cross and come along
Behind me,
You are not worthy of me.
Whoever finds his soul will lose it,
Whoever loses his soul, because of me, will find it.

10.37–39

A CUP OF COOL WATER FOR A CHILD

Whoever accepts you, accepts me.
Whoever accepts me, accepts the one who sent me.
Whoever accepts a prophet in the name of the prophet
Will have the reward of a prophet,
And whoever receives a just person in the name
Of a just person
Will have the reward of the just.
And whoever gives even a cup of cool water
To one of these children in the name of a student,[16]
I tell you none will go unrewarded.

10.40–42

IN THE WORDS OF OUR PROPHET YESHAYAHU[17]

The blind will see again and the lame walk,
The lepers are made clean and the deaf hear,
The dead are raised and the poor hear the good news.
Blessed is the one who has not stumbled because of me.

11.5–6

---

16 "Student" is in the Greek. "Disciple" is an entitling Latin upgrade and less appropriate for Jesus's immediate followers.
17 Isaiah.

IN THE DESERT

What did you go out to see?
A reed shaken by the wind?
A man dressed in soft robes?
Look, those who wear soft clothing
Are in the houses of the kings.
What did you go out to see?
A prophet? Yes, I tell you,
And he is more than a prophet.

The prophet Malachi wrote of him:
"See, I send my angel messenger before your face,
Who will prepare the way before you."
I say to you, no one arisen
Among us born of women
Is greater than Yohanan the Dipper.[18]
Yet in the kingdom of heaven
Who is least is greater than he is.

From the days of Yohanan the Dipper
The kingdom of heaven has been violated
And violent men seize it.
The prophets and all the law prophesied
That when Yohanan comes,
If you will accept it, Yohanan
Is the foretold Eliyahu.
Whoever has ears to hear, hear.

11.7–15

18 John the Baptist.

LIKE CHILDREN SITTING IN THE MARKETPLACE

But to what shall I compare our generation?
We are like children sitting in the marketplaces,
Calling out to one another, saying,
"We played the flute for you and you didn't dance.
We sang a dirge and you didn't mourn."
When Yohanan came he was not eating or drinking,
And they say, "He has a demon."
The earthly son came eating and drinking,
And they say, "Look at that glutton and drunk,
A friend of tax collectors and sinners,"
Yet wisdom is justified by her deeds.

11.16–19

REVEALED TO LITTLE CHILDREN

I praise you, lord of the sky and of the earth,
Because you have hidden these things from the wise
And the learned,
And revealed them to little children.

11.25

FATHER AND SON

Yes, father, in this way it was pleasing to you.
All things were given to me by my father,
And no one knows the son but the father,

And no one knows the father but the son
And any to whom the son wishes to reveal it.

11.26–27

Rest for Your Souls

Come to me, all who labor and are sorely burdened,
And I will give you rest.
Take my yoke upon you and learn from me
Because I am gentle and humble in heart,
And you will find rest for your souls
For my yoke is easy and my burden is light.

11.28–30

The Lord of the Shabbat

Have you not read what David did
When he and his companions were hungry?
How he went into the house of God
And ate the bread for the presentation,[19]
Which he was not permitted to eat,
Nor were those who were with him,
For that bread was for the priests alone?
Haven't you read in the law that priests in Temple
Break the Shabbat by their labors,

---

19 Twelve consecrated loaves of bread, changed weekly, set out in the synagogue as a symbol of communion with God. Also called "the bread of presence."

Yet they must be held innocent?
I tell you here is something greater than the Temple,
If you knew what our prophet Hoshea
Meant by "I wish mercy and not sacrifice,"
You would not condemn the innocent.
The lord of Shabbat is the earthly son.

12.3–8

A Sheep in a Pit on Shabbat

If you had only a single sheep
And it fell on Shabbat into a pit,
Wouldn't you grab it and pull it out?
A person is worth more than a sheep.
On the Shabbat one can do good.

12.11–12

My Love in Him in Whom My Soul Delights

Look, here is the servant I have chosen,
My love in whom my soul delights.[20]
I will place my spirit in him
And he will announce judgment for the foreigners.[21]
He will not quarrel or shout;
No one will hear his voice in the main streets.
He will not break a bruised reed
Or quench a smoking wick of flax

---

20 This line is the theme of the Song of Songs.
21 Gentiles.

Until he brings in the victory of judgment.
In his name the foreigners will hope.

12.18–21

A KINGDOM DIVIDED AGAINST ITSELF

Every kingdom divided against itself turns into a desert,
And every city or house divided against itself will not stand.

12.25

CASTING OUT DEMONS

If through Baal Zebul I cast out the demons,
Through whom do your sons cast them out?
Therefore they will be your judges.
But if through the spirit of God I cast out the demons,
The kingdom of God has come to you.

12.27–28

FRUIT, VIPERS, AND WORDS

Either make the tree good and its fruit good
Or make the tree bad and its fruit bad,
Because from the fruit the tree is known.
Offspring of vipers, how can you speak of the good
When you are evil?

The mouth speaks from an abundance in the heart.
The good person from a good storehouse draws good,
The evil one from an evil storehouse draws evil.
But I tell you that each idle word you utter
You will account for on the day of judgment,
For by your words you will be justified
And by your words you will be condemned.

12.33–37

THE SIGN OF YONAH[22]

A corrupt and adulterous generation asks for a sign
But no sign will be given to it
Except for the sign of Yonah the prophet.
For as Yonah was in the belly of the sea monster
Three days and three nights, so three days and three nights,
The earthly son will be in the heart of the earth. .
The men of Nineveh will stand up on the day of judgment
Of this generation, and they will condemn it,
Because they repented with the preaching of Yonah,
And look, there is more than Yonah here.
The Queen of the South[23] will rise on the day of judgment
Of this generation, and they will condemn it,
Because she came from the ends of the earth to listen
To the wisdom of Shlomoh,[24]
And look, there is one greater than Shlomoh here.

12.39–42

22 Jonah
23 The Queen of Sheba.
24 Solomon.

PARABLE OF THE SOWER

Look, a sower went out to sow
And as he was scattering the seed,
Some of the grain fell on the path
And some birds came and ate it.
Other seed fell on stony ground
Where there was not much soil
And the grain sprang up quickly,
For the soil had no depth.
But when the sun came up
The seedlings were parched
And, having no roots, withered.
Some fell among the thorns
And the thorns grew and choked them.
But some fell on good earth and bore fruit.
A hundredfold and sixty and thirty.
Whoever has ears to hear, hear.

13.3–9

WHY DO I SPEAK IN PARABLES?

You are given a knowledge of the secrets
Of the kingdom of heaven,
But that knowledge is not given to them.

When one has, more is granted.
When one has not, that little is taken away.

So I talk to them in parables,
For while they see, they do not see,
And while they hear, they do not hear or understand.

13.11–13

UNDERSTANDING WITH THE HEART

You hear, yet in hearing, you do not understand
And you see, yet in seeing, you do not see.

For the heart of this people has become calloused
And with their ears they hear poorly and their eyes are
    closed,

Otherwise they might see with their eyes,
And hear with their ears

And with their heart understand and turn
And I would heal them.[25]

But blessed are your eyes because they see
And your ears because they hear.

I say to you that many prophets and good people
Have longed to see what you see and did not see it,
And to hear what you hear and did not hear it.

13.14–17

25 Isa. 6.9–10.

PARABLE OF THE ASTUTE FARMER AND HIS FIELD WITH WEEDS SOWN MYSTERIOUSLY AMID THE WHEAT

The kingdom of heaven is like the man
Who sowed good seed in his field
And while his household was sleeping
His enemy came and sowed weeds amid the wheat
And disappeared.
When the plants grew and bore fruit
The weeds appeared.
Slaves came to the master of the house,
And asked him,
"Sir, did you not sow good seed in the field?
Where do the weeds come from?"
The master told them, "My enemy did this."
"Do you want us to go and pull them out?"
Said the slaves.
"No, in pulling the weeds you would uproot the wheat.
Let both grow together until the harvest.
Then at harvest I'll tell the reapers,
'First pull the weeds and tie them in bundles to burn,
And store the wheat in my granary.' "

13.24–30

THE MUSTARD SEED AND THE BIRDS

He set another parable before them, saying,
    The kingdom of heaven is like a mustard seed
    That someone took and planted in the field,

That is the smallest among all the seeds
But when it grows it is the greatest of the green shrubs
And becomes a tree
So birds of the sky can come and nest in its branches.

13.31–32

THE YEAST OF HEAVEN

The kingdom of heaven is like yeast
A woman hid in three measures of flour
So that the dough was leavened and rose.

13.33

OPENING THE HIDDEN

I open my mouth in parables,
I will pour out what has been hidden since the creation.[26]

13.35

PARABLE OF THE WEED GIVEN LIGHT

The one who sows the good seed is the earthly son
And the field is the cosmos,

The good seeds are the children of the kingdom,
But the weeds are the children of the evil one,

26 Ps. 78.2.

And the enemy who sowed them is the devil.
The harvest is the end of an age,

And the reapers are angels.
Then as the weeds are pulled up and burned in the fire

So it will be at the end of the age.
The earthly son will send out his angels

And they will gather from his kingdom
All scandalous things and those practicing lawlessness

And cast them into the furnace of fire
Where there will be weeping and gnashing of teeth.

Then the just will shine like the sun
In the kingdom of the father.

Whoever has ears to hear, hear.

13.37–43

THE TREASURE

The kingdom of heaven is like treasure
Hidden in a field,
Which someone finds and conceals,
And out of joy
Goes away and sells everything he ever bought
And buys that field.

13.44

THE PEARL

The kingdom of heaven
Is like a merchant seeking fine pearls.
After finding one precious pearl he sells everything
He has and buys that pearl.

13.45–46

THE LAST CATCH

The kingdom of heaven is like a net
Cast into the sea and catching every kind of fish.
When it is full and they drag it up on the shore
They lay it down and put the good fish in baskets,
But the rotted ones they throw out.

So it will be at the end of the age.
The angels will come and separate the evil from the just
And will cast the evil into the furnace of fire,
Where there will be weeping and gnashing of teeth.

13.47–50

THE LEARNED SCHOLAR

Every scholar who has knowledge
Of the kingdom of heaven
Is like a master of a household,
Who chooses the new and the old
From the storehouse of the treasures.

13.52

PROPHET WITHOUT HONOR

A prophet is not dishonored
Except in his own country and house.

13.57

WALKING ON THE WATERS OF THE SEA

Take heart.
It is I.
Do not be afraid.

14.27

WORSHIPING GOD IN A HOLLOW WAY

This people honors me with their lips,
But their heart is remote.
They worship me in a hollow way.
Their teachings are the rules of men.

15.8–9

THE BLIND

Every plant that my heavenly father has not planted
Will be uprooted.
Leave them. They are blind guides of the blind.

When the blind lead the blind,
They both fall into a pit.

15.13–14

FOR HELPING A CANAANITE WOMAN WHOSE DAUGHTER IS TORMENTED

I was sent here solely for the lost sheep
Of the house of Yisrael.

15.24

BREAD OF THE CHILDREN

It is not good to take the children's bread
And throw it to the dogs.

15.26

BREAD FOR FOUR THOUSAND ON THE SHORE

I pity the crowd. They have stayed with me
For three days and have nothing to eat.
I don't wish to send them away hungry
For fear they will collapse on their way.

15.32

THE KEYS OF THE KINGDOM

You are blessed, Shimon bar Yonah.[27]
It was not flesh and blood that revealed to you this vision
But my father who is in the heavens.
And I tell you that you are Kefa the rock
And upon this rock I will build my church
And the gates of Gei Hinnom will not overpower it.
I will give you the keys of the kingdom of the skies,
And whatever you close upon the earth
Will be closed in the heavens,
And whatever you open on the earth
Will be open in the heavens.

16.17–19

LOSING LIFE TO FIND THE SOUL

If you wish to be my follower,
Deny yourself,
Take up the cross and follow me.[28]

If you wish to save your soul
You will lose it.

If you lose your soul because of me,
You will find it.

---

27 Simon son of Jonah. The name "Kefa" in Aramaic/Hebrew means "rock." "Kefa" in Greek is "Petros," also meaning "rock" or "stone."In English "Petros" becomes "Peter." Hence Simon Peter was originally Shimon Kefa.

28 "Take up the cross" reflects a theme of later Christianity but not of this moment before the crucifixion. The call to "follow me" echoes through every moment, from the first words of Mark.

What good is it to gain the whole world
And forfeit your soul?

What will you give
In exchange for your soul?

The earthly son will come,
With his angels

In the glory of his father
And reward you by your deeds.

Some of you who stand here
Will not taste death

Until you see the earthly son
Coming in his kingdom.

16.24–28

ON A HIGH MOUNTAIN YESHUA IS TRANSFIGURED,
HIS FACE SHINES LIKE THE SUN, HIS CLOTHING IS
WHITE LIKE LIGHT,[29] AND FROM A SHINING CLOUD
COVERING THEM IN SHADOW, A VOICE SPEAKS

This is my son
Whom I love,
In whom I am happy.
Hear him.

17.5

---

29 Yeshua's transfiguration on the mountain.

WHEN HIS TERRIFIED STUDENTS FALL ON THEIR FACES, YESHUA TOUCHES THEM

Arise
And do not be afraid.

Speak to no one of the vision
Until the earthly son is raised from the dead.

17.7, 9

WILL MESSIANIC ELIYAHU COME HERE FIRST?

Eliyahu is coming and will set things right,
But I tell you that Eliyahu already came
And they did not know him and did with him as they cared
    to.
So the earthly son is to suffer at their hands.

17.11–12

YESHUA SPEAKS TO HIS STUDENTS ABOUT THEIR FAITH

You fail because of your poor faith.
I say to you, even if your faith is no bigger
Than a mustard seed,
When you say to the mountain to move
It will be moved
And nothing will be impossible for you.

17.20

Seizure Is Near

The earthly son is about to be handed over
To human hands and they will kill him
And on the third day he will be raised.

17.22–23

Safeguard Children from the Roman Taxman

Let the children be free of them.
But so as not to offend,
Go to the sea and cast
A fishhook into the waters
And take the first fish coming up,
Open its mouth.
You'll find a coin. Take it,
And give it to the taxman
For me and for you.

17.27

Becoming like Children

Unless you change and become like children,
You will never enter the kingdom of heaven.

But whoever becomes little like this child
Will be greatest in the kingdom of heaven,

And whoever in my name accepts a child
Like this one also accepts me,

But whoever leads one of these children to stumble
Who believes in me, for him it would be better

To hang a donkey's millstone around his neck
And be drowned in the depth of the sea.

18.3–6

LIVING ONE-EYED

If your hand or foot causes you to stumble,
Cut it off and throw it away from you.
It is better for you to enter life maimed or lame
Than to have two hands or two feet
And be hurled into eternal fire.
And if your eye causes you to stumble,
Rip it out and throw it away.
It is better for you to enter life one-eyed
Than to have two eyes
And be hurled into the Gei Hinnom of fire.

18.8–9

PARABLE OF A LOST SHEEP

Take care. Do not despise a little sheep.
I tell you that their angels in the air constantly gaze
At the face of my father who is in the heavens.
What seems right? If you have a hundred sheep
And one of them wanders away,
Will you not leave the ninety-nine on the mountain
And look for the one who wandered?
And if you happen to find it,
You are happier than over the ninety-nine
Who did not go astray.
So it is the wish of your father in the heavens
That none of the little ones be lost.

18.10–14

A BROTHER HURTING YOU

If your brother hurts you go to him alone
And show him the bruise. If you are heard
You have won the brother.
If unheard go with one or two witnesses
To confirm each word from your mouth.
If he doesn't hear go together to the synagogue
And if he will not listen to the synagogue
Let him be to you like a gentile or a tax collector.

18.15–17

On Earth as in Heaven

I tell you that whatever you close on earth
Will be locked up in heaven
And whatever you free on earth
Will be free in heaven.

Again I say,
If two agree about everything on earth they ask for,
It will be done for them by my father in the skies.
Where two or three come together in my name,
There I live among them.

18.18–20

How Many Times Do I Forgive a Brother?

I do not say to you as many as seven
But as many as seventy times seven.

18.22

Parable of a King and an Unforgiving Slave

So the kingdom of heaven is like a king
Who wished to settle accounts with his slaves.
As he was counting, a debtor of ten thousand talents
Was brought in who could not pay,
And his master ordered him to be sold,
And also his wife, children, and all they possessed

In order that his owner be repaid.
Then the slave fell on his knees before him
And said to him, "Delay your anger with me
And I will pay you back everything."
The lord had compassion for his slave
And he pardoned him and forgave the debt.
The slave went out and met a fellow slave,
Who owed him one hundred denarii,
And he seized him and choked him.
"Pay me back what you owe me," he said.
His fellow slave fell to the ground and begged him,
"Delay your anger, and I will repay you,"
But the freed slave was unwilling
And he left and threw him into prison
Until his fellow slave could pay the debt.
When the other slaves saw this they grieved immensely
And went and reported these things to their master.
The master called the wicked slave to him
And said, "I forgave you because you begged me.
Should you not have pity on your fellow slave
As I had compassion for you?"
And his master was angry and handed him
Over to the torturers in the prison
Until he paid back everything he owed.
In this way my father in heaven will handle
Each one of you unless you forgive
Your brother or sister from your heart.

18.23–35

LET THE LITTLE CHILDREN COME TO ME

Let the children be
And do not stop them from coming to me,
For this way is the kingdom in the heavens.

19.14

PERFECTION ON EARTH

If you wish to be perfect, go and sell
What belongs to you and give it to the poor,
And you will have a treasure in heaven.

Then come and follow me.

19.21

CALMING HIS STUDENTS

You know that the Roman rulers
Lord it over their people
And the high officials tyrannize them.
It will not be so for you,
For whoever among you wishes to be great
Will be your servant,
And whoever among you wishes to be first
Will be your slave.
So the earthly son did not come to be served
But to serve and to give his own life
For the redemption of the many.

20.25–28

ENTERING YERUSHALAYIM ON A COLT

Go on into the village ahead of you
And soon you will find a donkey tethered
And her foal beside her.
Untie them and bring them to me.
And if anyone should say anything to you,
Say that their master needs them,
And he will send them at once.

21.2–3

RIDING ON A DONKEY

Say to the daughter of Zion,
Look, your king is coming to you,
Modest and riding on a donkey
And with a colt, the foal of the donkey.

21.5

DRIVING THE TRADERS AND DOVE SELLERS FROM THE TEMPLE

"My house will be called a house of prayer,"
But you have made it a den of robbers.[30]

21.13

30 Isa. 56.7; Jer. 7.11.

Cursing and Drying Up the Fig Tree

If you have faith and do not doubt,
Not only what happened to the fig tree
Will be in your domain,
But you can say to the mountain,
Rise up and hurl yourself into the sea,
And it will be done.
All things you ask for in prayer with faith
You will receive.

21.21–22

Prophecy of the Temple Stones Thrown Down

Nothing here will escape destruction. No stone
Upon a stone will not be thrown down.

24.2

Coming of the Earthly Son

And suddenly after the suffering of those days,
The sun will be darkened
And the moon not give its light
And the stars fall out of heaven
And the powers of the heavens be shaken.
Then the sign of the earthly son will shine in the sky,
And all the tribes of the earth will beat themselves in
    mourning

And they will see
   The earthly son coming on the clouds
   In the high air
   With power and multiple glory,[31]
And he will send out his angels with a great ram horn blast
And they will gather the chosen ones from the four winds,
From one peak of heaven to the other peak.

24.29–31

LESSON OF THE FIG TREE ABOUT THE COMING OF THE EARTHLY SON

From the fig tree learn the parable,
When its branch is already tender and issues leaves
You know that summer is near.
So when you too see all these things,
You know that he is near.
As to that day and hour, no one knows.
Not angels in the air, nor the son.
None but the father alone.

For as the days of Noah came,
So will the coming of the earthly son.
For as in those days before the flood,
They were eating and drinking, marrying husbands and
   wives
Until the day Noah went into the ark,
And they knew nothing until the flood came

---

31 Dan. 7.13–14.

And carried everything away,
So will be the coming of the earthly son.

Then two men will be in the field:
One is taken away and one is left.
Two women will be grinding flour at the mill:
One is taken away and one is left.
So be watchful, since you don't know on what day
Your lord is coming.
But you know that if the master of the house
Had known at what hour of the night the thief was coming,
He would have kept awake
And not allowed his house to be broken into.
Therefore, you also must keep awake,
For in an hour unknown to you comes the earthly son.

24.32–33, 36–44

TEN VIRGINS AND THEIR OIL LAMPS

Then the kingdom of heaven can be compared
To ten young virgins who picked up their lamps
And went out to meet the bridegroom.
Five of them were foolish and five were wise.
The fools took their lamps but not the oil.
The clever ones took flasks of oil with their lamps,
But when the bridegroom was delayed,
The virgins all grew drowsy and fell asleep.

In the middle of the night there was a shout.
"Look, it is the bridegroom. Go out to meet him."

Then the women woke and trimmed their lamps,
But the fools said to the wise, "Give us some
Of your oil, because our lamps are going out."
But the wise ones answered, saying, "No,
There would never be enough for us and you.
Better go out to the merchants and buy some for yourselves."

And while they were gone to buy the oil,
The groom came and the virgins ready with light
Went with the groom into the wedding,
And the door was shut. Soon the others came crying,
"Lord, lord, open the door to us!"
But the master answered them in turn,
"I tell you, I don't know you." Be watchful,
For you do not know the day or the hour.

25.1–12

WHEN SHE POURED MYRRH ON MY BODY
IN THE HOUSE OF THE LEPER

Why are you troubling this woman
Who has done a good thing for me?
The poor you always have with you,
But me you will not always have.
When she poured myrrh on my body,
She prepared me for my burial.
Amain, I say to you, where in all the world
The good news is proclaimed,
What she has done will be told
In memory of this woman.

26.10–13

Planning the Seder in an Upper Room

Go into the city to a certain man and tell him,
"The teacher says: My time is near.
And I will celebrate the Pesach at your house
with my students."

26.18

One of You Will Betray

I tell you that one of you will betray me.

The one who has dipped his hand
In the bowl with me will betray me.
Yes, the earthly son departs
As the prophet wrote of him,
But agony is prepared for him
Who betrays the earthly son.
Better had he not been born!

26.21, 23–24

Yeshua Breaking the Matzot Bread for His Students

Take it and eat.
It is my body.

Drink from this cup, all of you.
It is my blood of the covenant,

Poured out to forgive
The many of sin.

I will no longer drink this fruit of the vine
Until that day I drink it new with you.

26.26–29

BEFORE THE COCK CROWS TWICE YOU WILL ALL DESERT ME

You will all desert me this night.
As it is written in Zeharyahu,
I will strike down the shepherd
And the sheep of his flock will be scattered.
But after I am raised up,
I will go ahead of you to the Galil.

26.31–32

DURING THE NIGHT TO SHIMON KEFA

During this night before the cock crows
You will deny me three times.

26.34

TERROR AND PRAYER AT GAT SHMANIM[32]

Sit down here while I go over there to pray.
My soul is in anguish to the point of death.
Stay here and keep awake with me.

26.36, 38

YESHUA PRAYS PROSTRATE, HIS FACE ON THE EARTH

My father, if it is possible,
Let this cup pass from me,
But not as I wish, but as you wish.

26.39

TO SHIMON KEFA WHO HAS FALLEN ASLEEP

Were you not strong enough to stay awake
With me for one hour? Stay awake and pray
That you are not brought to the test.
The spirit is eager but the flesh is weak.

26.40–41

32 Gethsemane.

YESHUA GOES OFF AGAIN AND PRAYS

My father, if this cup cannot pass from me
Without my drinking it,
Let your will be done.

26.42

REBUKING AND WARNING HIS STUDENTS

Are you still asleep and resting?
Look, the hour is near, and the earthly son
Will be betrayed into the hands of sinners.
Wake up, let us go.
Look, the one betraying me is near.

26.45–46

YESHUA TELLS YEHUDA[33] WHAT HE MUST DO[34]

Friend, do what you are here to do.

26.50

33 Judas.
34 This phrase suggests the other version of the story of Judas, where Jesus urges
Judas to denounce him. See the Gospel of Judas, in *The Restored New Testament*.

To One with Yeshua Who Has Cut Off the Ear of the High Priest's Slave

Put your sword back into its place,
For all who draw the sword will die by the sword.
Do you think I don't have the power to call on my father
To send me at once twelve legions of angels?
How else would the scriptures be fulfilled
That say in this way these things must happen?[35]

26.52–54

Yeshua to the Crowd

Have you come to arrest me with swords and clubs
As if I were a robber?
Day after day I sat in the Temple, teaching,
And you did not take hold of me.
All this is happening so the scriptures
Of the prophets are fulfilled.

26.55–56

Yeshua Replies to the High Priest Who Has Asked Him, Are You the Mashiah, the Son of God?

You said it. But I say to you,
From now on you will see the earthly son

---

35 2 Kings 6.15–17; Ps. 24.8–10; Rev. 19.14.

Seated at the right hand of the power
And coming upon the clouds of the sky.[36]

26.64

PILATUS[37] THE GOVERNOR ASKS YESHUA, ARE YOU THE KING OF THE JEWS?

You say so.

27.11

DARKNESS AT NOON

Eli, Eli, lama sabachthani?[38]
My God, my God, why have you forsaken me?

27.46

YESHUA RISEN SPEAKS TO MIRYAM OF MAGDALA AND THE OTHER MIRYAM[39] ON THE ROAD NEAR HIS EMPTY TOMB

Do not fear. Go and tell my brothers and sisters
To go to the Galil and there they will see me.

28.10

36 Daniel 7.13, which he cites, reads, "I saw one like a person / coming upon the clouds of the sky."
37 Pilate.
38 Ps. 22.1. Jesus's words are in Hebrew.
39 Mary Magdalene and the other Mary.

Yeshua in the Galil[40] with His Students

To me was given all authority in heaven and on earth.
Go and make all nations into students,
Washing them in the name of the father and the son
And the holy spirit,
Teaching them to hold to all I have commanded you.
And know I am with you
All the days until the end of eternity.

28.18–20

40 Galilee.

LUKE
(Loukas)

The Gospel of Luke is the longest of the gospels, and, according to most commentators, the most skillfully constructed one, composed in an elegant Greek at times approaching classical Hellenistic Greek of the first century.

Perhaps the most original and beautiful passages in Luke—and there are no counterparts in the other gospels—are the annunciation moment (1.26–38), Mary's visit to Elizabeth (1.39–56), the nativity scene of the birth of Yeshua in the manger (2.1–7), and the parable of the Good Samaritan (10.29–37). Along with Luke's narrative genius, extraordinary poetry fills the pages of his book, including the painfully beautiful and moving "The Lost Son" ("The Prodigal Son"). Luke is also a major influence on other poets, including T. S. Eliot, whose "Song for Simeon" begins unforgettably:

> Lord, the Roman hyacinths are blooming in bowls and
> The winter sun creeps by the snow hills;
> The stubborn season has made stand.
> My life is light, waiting for the death wind,
> Like a feather on the back of my hand.
> Dust in sunlight and memory in corners
> Wait for the wind that chills towards the dead land.

The seminal influence of Luke has magnified the history of great English poetry. Luke is a supreme narrator and poet of the scriptures.

AFTER YOSEF AND MIRYAM FIND HIM AT AGE TWELVE IN THE TEMPLE, SITTING WITH AND QUESTIONING THE RABBIS

Why were you looking for me?
Did you not know I must be
In the house of my father the lord?

2.49

TO THE DEVIL TAUNTING HIM, "IF YOU ARE THE SON OF GOD, TELL THIS STONE TO BECOME BREAD"

As it is written in the Torah,
One does not live by bread alone.

4.4

SAYING YESHAYAHU'S[1] PROPHECY IN THE NATZERET SYNAGOGUE[2]

The spirit of the lord is upon me,
Through which he anointed me
To bring good news to the poor.
He sent me to preach release of captives
And vision to the blind,
To let the downtrodden go free,
To proclaim the year of the lord's favor.

4.18–19

1 Isaiah.
2 Isa. 61.1–2; 58.6.

ON LAKE GENNESARET WITH SHIMON KEFA

Go out into the deep waters
And drop your nets and fish.

Do not be afraid. From now on
You will be catching people.

5.4, 10

TO LEVI THE TAX COLLECTOR IN HIS BOOTH, PERSUADING HIM TO LEAVE EVERYTHING BEHIND

Follow me.

5.27

BLESSINGS SERMON ON THE PLAIN

Blessed are the poor
For yours is the kingdom of God.

Blessed are you who are hungry now
For you will be fed.

Blessed are you who weep now
For you will laugh.

Blessed are you when people hate you,
When they ostracize you and blame you

And cast your name about as evil because of the earthly son.
Be happy on that day and spring and leap,

For look, your reward is great in the sky.
For in the same way their fathers treated the prophets.

6.20–23

A PLAGUE ON THE RICH

But a plague on you the rich,
For you have received your consolation.

A plague on you who are filled now,
For you will hunger.

A plague on you who laugh now,
For you will mourn and weep.

A plague on you when all people speak well of you,
For so did their fathers treat the false prophets.

But I say to you who listen:

Love your enemies, do good to those who hate you,
And praise those who curse you.

6.24–28

SAYINGS OF LOVE AND ENEMIES

Praise those who curse you.
Pray for those who abuse you.

When one slaps you on the cheek,
Offer the other cheek as well.

From one who takes your coat,
Do not withhold your shirt.

To all who ask you,
Give what you have.

From one who takes what is yours,
Ask nothing back.

As you wish people to do for you,
Do for them.

If you love those who love you, what grace is yours?
Even sinners love those who love them.

And if you do good to those who do good,
What grace is yours? Sinners do the same.

If you lend to those from whom you hope return,
    what grace is yours?
Even sinners lend to sinners for a like return.

But love your enemies and do good,
And when you loan, ask nothing in return.

Your reward will be great.
You will be the children of the highest.

He is kind to the ungrateful as he is to the cunning.
Be compassionate as your father is compassionate.

6.28–36

SAYINGS OF JUDGMENT

Do not judge and you will not be judged.
Do not condemn and you will not be condemned.
Forgive and you will be forgiven.
Give and you will be given.

A good measure of wheat shaken, packed down
And overflowing will be placed in your lap,
Since the measure of what you give
Will be the measure of your return.

6.37–38

NO GOOD TREE BEARS ROTTEN FRUIT

No good tree bears rotten fruit,
And so no rotten tree bears good fruit.
Each tree is known by its own fruit.

Not from thorns are figs gathered
Nor from brambles are grapes picked.

The good person from the good treasure house
Of the heart brings forth good,
And the cunning person out of cunning brings forth
    cunning.

Out of the fullness of the heart, the mouth speaks.

6.43–45

PARABLE OF THE HOUSE AND FOUNDATION

Why do you call me "lord, lord,"
And do not do what I say?
When anyone comes to me and hears my words
And does them,
I will show you who that person is like.

That person is like the man building a house
Who dug and went down deep and laid a foundation on
    rock.
The flood came and the river burst against that house
And it was not strong enough to shake it,
Because the house was well built.
But one who hears and does not do
Is like the man who builds a house on the earth
Without any foundation,
Against which the river bursts
And at once the house collapses under the river
And the ruin of that house is great.

6.46–49

HELPING THE BLIND, THE LAME, AND THE LEPERS

The blind see again, the lame walk, lepers are cleansed,
The deaf hear, the dead arise,
The poor are told good news.
And blessed is one who does not stumble
And fall into wrong because of me.

7.22–23

TELLING THE CROWD ABOUT YOHANAN

What did you come into the desert to see?
A reed shaken by the wind?
But what did you come out to look at?
A man dressed in soft clothing?
Look, those who are in splendid clothing
And luxury are in the palaces of the kings.
But what did you go out to see? A prophet?
Yes, I tell you. And more than a prophet,
This is he about whom Malachi writes,[3]
"Look, I send my messenger before your face
Who will prepare the way before you."
I tell you, among those born of women
There is no one greater than Yohanan.
But there is one who is the very least,
Yet in the kingdom of God greater than he.

7.24–28

---

3 Mal. 3.1 and Exod. 23.20.

THEY CALL ME A GLUTTON AND A DRUNK

What are the people of this generation
And to whom shall I compare them?
They are children in the marketplace,
Sitting and calling out to each other, who say,
    We played the flute for you
    And you didn't dance.
    We sang a dirge
    But you didn't weep.
Yohanan the Dipper came and ate no bread
And drank no wine, and you say, "He has a demon."
The earthly son comes and eats and drinks
And you say, "Look, this man is a glutton and a drunk,
A friend of tax collectors and sinners."
But wisdom is proved right by all her children.

7.31–35

A LOVING PROSTITUTE WHO WASHES YESHUA'S FEET WITH HER TEARS AND DRIES THEM WITH HER HAIR

Do you see this woman?
I came into your house.
You did not give me water for my feet,

But she washed my feet with her tears.
You gave me no kiss,
But from the time I came in
She has not stopped kissing my feet.

You did not anoint my head with olive oil,
But she anointed my feet with myrrh.

Therefore, I tell you, her many sins
Are forgiven, for she loved much.
But one who is forgiven little, loves little.

7.44–47

LAMP AND LIGHT

No one lights a lamp and puts it in a jar
Or under the bed.
One puts it on a lampstand
So that those who come in may see the light.
For nothing is hidden that will not become visible,
And nothing is obscure that will not be known
And come into the light.

8.16–17

YESHUA IS TOLD THAT HIS MOTHER AND BROTHERS ARE STANDING OUTSIDE AND WISH TO SEE HIM

My mother and my brothers are those
Who hear the word of God and do it.

8.21

CURING THE BLEEDING WOMAN

Someone touched me. I felt the power
Go out from me.

Daughter, your faith has saved you.
Go in peace.

8.46, 48

YOUR DAUGHTER IS DEAD

Do not be afraid. Only believe
And she will be saved.

Do not weep. She did not die
But is sleeping.

Child, get up!

8.50, 52, 54

INSTRUCTIONS FOR THE TWELVE ON THE ROAD

Take nothing for the road,
No staff, no bag, no bread, no silver,
Not even two tunics.
Whatever house you go into, stay there,
And leave from there.
And whoever does not receive you,

As you go out of that city shake the dust
From your feet
In testimony against them.

9.3–5

LOSING LIFE TO FIND THE SOUL

Whoever wants to save the soul
Will lose it,
But whoever loses the soul because of me
Will save it.

What benefit is there to gain the whole world
And lose or punish yourself?

9.24–25

GREATNESS AND THE CHILD

Whoever receives this child in my name
Receives me,
And whoever receives me receives the one
Who sent me.
Whoever is smallest among you all,
That one is great.

9.48

HOMELESS

Foxes have holes and birds of the sky have nests,
But the earthly son has no place to lay his head.

9.58

SEVENTY NAKED LAMBS ON THE ROAD

The harvest is abundant, but the workers few.
So ask the master of the harvest
To send out workers into his harvest.
Go forth. Look, I send you as lambs
Into the midst of wolves.
Carry no purse or bag or sandals,
And greet no one along the road.

Whatever house you enter, first say, "Peace to this house."
And if a child of peace is there,
Your peace will stay with that one.
And if not, it will return to you.
Remain in the same house, eating and drinking with them,
For the worker deserves his wages.

Don't wander from house to house.
And when you go into any city and they receive you,
Eat what they set before you
And heal those who are sick and say to them,
"The kingdom of God is near."

10.2–9

RETURN OF THE SEVENTY LAMBS

I saw Satan falling from the sky like a flash of lightning.
Look, I have given you authority to walk on snakes
And scorpions,
And over all the power of the enemy,
And nothing will ever harm you.
But do not rejoice that the spirits submit to you.
Rejoice that your names are written in heaven.

10.18–20

PARABLE OF THE GOOD SHOMRONI[4]

A man was going down from Yerushalayim[5]
To Yeriho[6] and fell into the hands
Of robbers. They stripped him and beat him
And went away leaving him half dead.
By chance a priest went down the same road
And when he saw him he passed by on the other side.
And a Levite also came by and saw him
And passed by on the other side.
But a Shomroni on his journey came near
And when he saw him he pitied him.
He went to him and bound his wounds
And poured olive oil and wine over him,
And set him on his own beast, and took him
To an inn where he cared for him.

4 Samaritan.
5 Jerusalem.
6 Jericho.

And on the next day he took out and gave
Two denarii to the innkeeper and said,
"Take care of him and what costs you still may have,
I will repay when I return."
Which of the three seems to you the neighbor
Of the man who fell before the robbers?

10.30–36

MIDNIGHT FRIEND AND BREAD

Who among you has a friend and will go
To him at midnight and say to him,
"Friend, lend me three loaves, because my friend
Has come in from the road to my house
And I have nothing to set before him."
And the one inside answers and says,
"Don't bring me troubles. I've already locked
The door and my children are in bed.
I cannot get up to give you anything."
I tell you, even if he will not get up
And give it to him because he is a friend,
Yet he will wake up and give him
What he needs because of his persistence.

11.5–8

SON ASKING FOR A FISH

Who among you has a son who would ask his father for a
   fish
And instead of fish he will give him a snake?
Or even if he asked for an egg,
Will he give him a scorpion?
If then you who are cunning know how to give
Good gifts to your children,
By how much more will the father from the sky
Give holy spirit to those who ask him?

11.11–13

HOW I CAST OUT DEMONS

You say I cast out demons through Baal Zebul.
But if through Baal Zebul I cast out demons,
By whom do your sons cast them out?
So they will be your judges.
Yet if through the finger of God I cast out demons,
Then the kingdom of God has come to you.

11.18–20

STRONG MAN AND PEACE

When a strong man, fully armed, guards his own castle,
His possessions are in peace.
But when one stronger than he attacks and overpowers him,
He takes off the armor in which he trusted
And gives away his plunder.

11.21–22

WHO IS NOT WITH ME

One who is not with me is against me
And who does not gather with me scatters.

11.23

WANDERINGS OF AN UNCLEAN SOUL

When an unclean spirit goes out of a person,
It goes through waterless places seeking a place to rest,
And finding none, it says,
"I shall return to my house from which I came."
And when an unclean spirit goes back,
It finds the house swept and in order.
Then it goes and picks up other spirits slyer than itself,
Seven of them who all go in and live there,
And the last condition for that person
Is even worse than the beginning.

11.24–26

SIGN OF YONAH

This generation is a malicious generation.
It seeks a sign and it will be given no sign
Except for the sign of Yonah.
Just as Yonah became a sign to the people of Nineveh,
So is the earthly son for this generation.
The Queen of the South[7] will rise up
On the day of judgment with the men of this generation
And she will condemn them, for she came
From the ends of the earth to hear the wisdom of Shlomoh,[8]
And look, one greater than Shlomoh is here.
The men of Nineveh will rise up
On the day of judgment with this generation
And condemn it because they repented
On hearing the preaching of Yonah,
And look, one greater than Yonah is here.

11.29–32

LAMP ON A STAND

No one lights a lamp and puts it in a hidden place,
But on the lampstand
So that those who come in may see the light.
The lamp of the body is your eye.
When your eye is clear, then your whole body
Is filled with light.

7 Queen of Sheba.
8 Solomon.

But when it is clouded, then your body is darkness.
So if your whole body is filled with light,
With no part dark,
You will be all light as when the lamp illumines you
With its beams.

11.33–36

HIDDEN INTO LIGHT

There is nothing hidden that will not be revealed,
And nothing secret that will not be known.
What you have said in darkness will be heard in the light,
And what you said to the ear in inner rooms
Will be proclaimed on the housetops.

12.2–3

GOD'S MEMORY OF SPARROWS AND PENNIES

Are five sparrows not sold for two pennies?
And not one of them is forgotten before God.
But even the hairs of your head are all counted.
Do not fear.
You are worth more than many sparrows.

12.6–7

CONSIDER THE RAVENS OF THE SKY

So I tell you this. Do not worry about your life,
What you eat, about your body, or how you clothe yourself.
The soul is more than food and the body more than
   clothing.
Consider the ravens who do not sow or reap,
Who have no storehouse or barn,
And God feeds them.
How much more are you worth than the birds!

12.22–24

SETTING HEARTS ON THE KINGDOM

And look not for what you can eat and drink,
And do not worry.
All the nations of the world seek them,
But your father knows you are in need.
Seek only his kingdom
And these things will be added for you.
Little flock, do not fear, for your father
Is happy to give you the kingdom.

12.29–32

GIVE AND NO MOTH OR THIEF DESTROYS

Sell your possessions and give charities.
Make yourselves purses that never wear out,
Be an inexhaustible treasure in heaven

Where no thief comes near or moth destroys.
Where your treasure is,
There also will be your heart.

12.33–34

THE MASTER MAY COME AT ANY HOUR

Let your loins be girded about and the lamps burning
And be like people waiting for their master
When he comes back from the wedding,
So that when he comes and knocks
They will open for him at once.
Blessed are the slaves whom the lord
On his return finds wide awake.
Amain, I tell you, he will gird himself up
And have them recline to eat and he will come near
And he will serve them.
And if he comes in the second watch[9] or third watch[10]
And finds them alert, they will be blessed.
But know this. If the master of the house
Knew what time the thief was coming,
He would not have let his house be broken into.
Be ready, for the earthly son comes
In the hour when you least expect him.

12.35–40

9 Midnight.
10 Three in the morning.

I CAME WITH FIRE

I came to cast fire over the earth
And how I wish it were already ablaze!

12.49

I DO NOT BRING PEACE BUT DIVISION

Do you think I came to bring peace on earth?
No, I tell you, I came to bring division.
From now on there will be five in one house
Dissenting against two and two against three.
Father will be divided against son and son against father,
Mother against daughter and daughter against mother,
Mother-in-law against daughter-in-law
And daughter-in-law against mother-in-law.

12.51–53

READING RAIN CLOUDS AND PAYING DEBTS

When you see a cloud rising in the west,
At once you say a rain storm is coming.
And so it comes. When a south wind blows
You say it will be hot. You hypocrites!
The face of the earth and the sky you know
How to read. Why don't you know how to read
These times? Why don't you judge on your own
What is right? As you go with your opponent

To the magistrate, try on the way there
To reconcile with him, or you may be dragged
Before the judge, and the judge will hand you
Over to the bailiff and the bailiff throw you
In jail. I tell you, you will never get out
Of there until you pay back the last penny.

12.54–59

PARABLE OF THE BARREN FIG TREE

A man had a fig tree planted in his vineyard
And he went looking for fruit on it
And found none. He said to the gardener,
"Look, for three years I have come looking
For fruit on this tree and have found none.
Cut it down. Why should it be wasting the soil?"
But he answered and said to him, "Sir, let it go
For another year while I dig around it
And throw manure on it. Then it may bear fruit
In the future. And if not, cut it down."

13.6–9

MUSTARD SEED AND THE KINGDOM OF GOD

What is the kingdom of God like
And to what shall I compare it?
It is like a mustard seed that a man threw

Into his garden and it grew into a tree,
And the birds of the sky nested in its branches.

13.18–19

YEAST AND THE KINGDOM OF GOD

What is the kingdom of God?
It is yeast a woman took and concealed
In three measures of wheat until it was all leavened.

13.20–21

THE NARROW GATE

Struggle to go in through the narrow door,
Because many, I tell you, will try to get in
And will not succeed, for once the master
Of the house wakens and shuts the door,

You will begin to stand outside and knock,
Saying, Lord, open for us. And he will answer,
Saying to you, I do not know you or where
You come from. Then you will begin to say,

We ate and drank with you, and you taught
In our broad streets. Then he will tell you,
I do not know where you come from.
Go away from me, all you workers of iniquity!

There will be the weeping and gnashing of teeth
When you see Avraham[11] and Yitzhak[12] and Yaakov[13]
And all the prophets in the kingdom of God,
But you will be cast alone outside.

And they will come from east and west
And from north and south and they will recline
At a table in the kingdom of God. And look,
The last will be first and the first will be last.

13.24–30

HEALING A MAN WITH DROPSY ON SHABBAT

Who among you who has a son or an ox
Fallen into a well
Will not lift it out immediately
On the day of Shabbat?

14.5

CHOOSING A PLACE AT THE TABLE

When you are invited by someone to
A wedding, do not recline at the table
In the place of honor, for possibly one
With more honors than you has been invited by him.

11 Abraham.
12 Isaac.
13 Jacob.

Then he who invited you will say to you,
"Give up your place," and you will slip
With shame into the very last place.
But when you are invited, go and take
The lowest place so when your host comes
He will say to you, "Friend, move up higher."
Then glory will come to you before all
Who are reclining at the table with you,
Because all who exalt themselves high
Will be humbled low, and those who choose
To humble themselves will be exalted.

14.8–11

Yeshua Tells the Host about Choosing Guests at Your Table

When you prepare a lunch or supper,
Do not invite your friends or your brothers
Or your relations or rich neighbors,
For possibly they will invite you in return
And it will be a repayment to you.
When you prepare a banquet invite
The poor, the crippled, the lame, the blind.
Then you will be blessed, for they have not means
To repay you, but you will be repaid
At the resurrection of the good.

14.12–14

HATE YOUR FATHER AND MOTHER, RENOUNCE EVERYTHING AND FOLLOW ME

If someone comes to me and does not hate
His father and mother and wife and children
And brothers and sisters and even life itself,
He cannot be my student. Whoever does not
Carry the cross and follow me cannot be my student.

14.26–27

TASTE OF SALT

Salt is good. But if salt has lost its taste
How can it be seasoned?
It is not fit for the land or a dunghill.
They throw it out.
Whoever has ears to hear, hear.

14.34–35

PARABLE OF THE LOST SHEEP

Who among you who has a hundred sheep
And has lost one of them will not leave
The ninety-nine in the wilderness
And go after the one lost until it is found?
Once he finds it he sets it on his shoulders
And is happy. And when he comes home
He calls his friends and neighbors together
And tells them, "Celebrate with me,

For I have found my sheep that was lost."
I say to you there will be more joy
In heaven over one sinner who repents
Than over ninety-nine of the just
Who have no need of repentance.

15.4–7

PARABLE OF THE LOST DRACHMA

Or what woman who has ten drachmas[14]
If she loses one will not light a lamp
And sweep the house and search carefully
Until she finds it? And finding it, she calls
Together friends and neighbors, saying,
"Celebrate with me, for I have found the coin
I lost." So I tell you, there is joy
Among the angels over one sinner who repents.

15.8–10

PARABLE OF THE LOST SON[15]

There was a man who had two sons.
The younger said to his father, "Father,
Give me the share of the property
That will belong to me." So he divided
His resources between them. And not

---

14 The drachma was a Greek silver coin worth about a day's wage.
15 Commonly called "The Prodigal Son."

Many days later the younger son
Got all his things together and went off
To a far country and there he squandered
His substance by riotous living.

When he had spent everything he had,
There came a severe famine throughout
That country, and he began to be in need.
And he went and hired out to a citizen
Of that land, who sent him to his fields
To feed the pigs. He longed to be fed
On the pods the pigs were eating, but no one
Gave him anything. He came to himself
And said, "How many of the day laborers
Of my father have bread left over and here
I'm starving and dying. I will rise up
And go to my father and I will say to him,
'Father, I have sinned against heaven
And before you. I am no longer worthy
To be called your son. Make me
Like one of your hired hands.' "
And he rose up and went to his father.

While he was still far in the distance,
His father saw him and was filled
With compassion, his tears fell on his neck
And he kissed him. And the son said to him,
"Father, I have sinned against heaven
And before you. I am no longer worthy
To be called your son." But his father said
To his slaves, "Quick, bring out the finest robe
And put it on him, and give him a ring

For his hand and sandals for his feet.
And bring the fatted calf, slaughter it,
And let us eat and celebrate, for my son
Was dead and he came back to life,
He was lost and he has been found."
And they began to celebrate.

Now the older son was in the fields
And as he drew near the house he heard
Music and dancing. And he called over
One of his slaves and asked what was going on.
He told him, "Your brother is here,
And your father has slaughtered the fatted calf
Because he took him back in good health."

The son was angry and did not want to go in,
But his father came out and pleaded with him.
But he answered and said to his father,
"Look, so many years I have served you
And never disobeyed an order of yours,
And for me you never gave a young goat
So I could celebrate with my friends.
But when this son of yours came, who ate up
Your property with prostitutes, for him
You slaughtered the fatted calf."

Then his father said, "Child, you are always with me,
And everything that is mine is yours,
But we must be happy and celebrate.
Your brother was a dead man and he has come alive,
And he was lost and has been found."

15.11–32

FAITHFUL IN RICHES

One who is faithful in the little thing
Is faithful in the bigger, and one who is
Dishonest in the little is also dishonest
In the bigger. So if you have not
Been faithful with dishonest wealth,
Who will believe in you for true riches?
And if you have not been faithful
With what belongs to another,
Who will give you what is your own?

16.10–12

DILEMMA OF TWO MASTERS

No house slave can serve two masters.
Either he will hate one and love the other
Or be devoted to one and despise the other.
You cannot serve God and mammon.[16]

16.13

WHEN YOUR BROTHER DOES WRONG

Look at yourselves. If your brother does wrong
And repents, forgive him. And if he does wrong
Seven times a day against you and seven times
Turns around to say, "I repent," forgive him.

17.3–4

---

16 One fond of money.

Faith Uprooting a Black Mulberry Tree

If you have faith like a grain of mustard seed
You could say to this black mulberry tree,
"Pluck yourself up by the roots and plant yourself
In the sea," and it would still obey you.

17.6

Coming of the Kingdom of God Mysteriously Inside

The kingdom of God is not coming
In an observable way,
Nor will people say, "Look, it is here!"
Or, "It is there!"
For look, the kingdom of God is inside you.

17.20–21

Majesty and Terror in the Apocalyptic Coming of the Earthly Son

The days are coming when you will long to see
One of the days of the earthly son,
And you will not see it.
And they will say to you, "Look, there!" or "Look, here!"
Do not go after them! Do not follow them!
For as lightning burns at one end of the sky
And then at the other end of the sky glistens,

So will be the coming of the earthly son.
But first he must suffer multiple wrongs
And be rejected by this generation.
And as it happened in the days of Noah,
So it will be in the days of the earthly son.
The people were eating, drinking, marrying,
And given away in marriage until the day
Noah went into the ark and the flood came
And destroyed all of them. It was the same
As in the days of Lot. They were eating,
Drinking, buying, selling, planting, building.
But on the day Lot went out of Sedom
It rained fire and sulfur from the sky
And destroyed everything. So it will be
On the day the earthly son is revealed.

On that day if a man is on the roof and his goods
Are in the house, let him not come down
To carry them away. And one in the field
Likewise let him not turn back for anything
Left behind. Remember the wife of Lot.
Whoever tries to preserve her life will lose it,
But whoever loses it will bring it to life.
I tell you, on that night there will be two men
In one bed. One will be taken, the other left.
There will be two women grinding meal
At the same place. One will be taken, the other left.

17.22–35

WHERE, LORD, WILL THESE THINGS OCCUR?

Where the corpse is, the vultures assemble.

17.37

LET THE CHILDREN COME TO ME

Let the children come to me
And do not stop them, for the kingdom of God
Belongs to them.

Whoever does not receive the kingdom of God
Like a child will never enter therein.

18.16–17

WHO CAN BE SAVED?

What is impossible for people
Is possible for God.

18.27

REWARDS FOR ABANDONING FAMILY FOR THE KINGDOM

There is no one who has left house or wife
Or parents or children for the kingdom of God
Who will not receive back many times more
In this age
And in the age to come of life everlasting.

18.29–30

I WILL DIE AND BE RISEN

Look, we are going up to Yerushalayim
And all that has been written by the prophets
About the earthly son will be fulfilled.
He will be handed over to the Romans
And they will mock and insult and spit on him,
And after scourging him they will kill him
And on the third day he will rise again.

18.31–33

BLIND BEGGAR IN YERIHO WHO ASKS YESHUA TO LET HIM SEE

See again. Your faith has healed you.

18.42

To Zakai,[17] a Rich Tax Collector Who Gave Half His Possessions to the Poor, Who Is a True Jew and Will Be Saved

Zakai, hurry and come down.
Today I must stay at your house.

Salvation has come to this house today,
Because you too are a son of Avraham.[18]
The earthly son came to seek and to save the lost.

19.5, 9–10

Entering Yerushalayim on a Colt

Go into the village just ahead
And as you enter you will find a tethered colt
On which no one has ever sat.
Untie it and bring it here.
If someone asks you, "Why are you untying it?"
You will say, "His master needs it."

19.30–31

Telling His Students to Speak Out

I tell you, if you are silent,
The stones will weep.

19.40

17 Zacchaeus.
18 "Son of Abraham" meant a true Jew and not one to be excluded from society because, as a tax collector, he was working for the Roman occupiers.

OF YAHWEH AND THE MASHIAH[19]

How can they say the mashiah is the descendant of David
When David himself says in Psalms:
    "Yahweh said to my lord,
    'Sit at my right side
    Till I have made your enemies your footstool?' "[20]
David calls him lord. How then can he be his son?

20.41–44

THE WIDOW'S COPPER COINS

This widow who is poor
Has cast in more than anyone else.
All of them put in gifts from their abundance
While she in her poverty cast in
All the pennies she had to live on.

21.2–4

DESTRUCTION OF THE TEMPLE FORETOLD

As for what you see,
The days will come
When there will be

19 Messiah.
20 Ps. 110.1.

Not one stone on a stone
Not thrown down.[21]

21.6

BEWARE OF FALSE MASHIAHS

Beware that you are not fooled.
Many will come in my name, saying, "I am he.
The time is near." Do not follow them.
When you hear about wars and uprisings,
Do not be alarmed, for these must happen first,
But the end will not come soon.
Nation will rise up against nation
And kingdom contend with kingdom.
There will be great earthquakes,
And in many places there will be famines
And plagues, and horrors,
And there will be great signs from the sky.

21.8–11

BETRAYAL AND PERSECUTIONS BECAUSE OF MY NAME

But before all these things, they will lay their hands on you
And persecute you
And turn you over to the temples and jails,

---

21 Reference is to the Romans' conquest of Jerusalem and burning of the Temple in
70 C.E.

And you will be brought before kings and governors,
Because of my name.
This will be your time to testify.
So keep in your hearts that you must not prepare
To defend yourselves,
For I will give you such a tongue and wisdom
That all those opposed to you
Will not resist or stand against you.

21.12–15

THOUGH PARENTS AND FRIENDS BETRAY AND KILL YOU, YOU GAIN YOUR SOULS

You will be betrayed even by parents
And brothers and relatives and friends,
And they will put some of you to death,
And you will be hated by all because of my name.
Yet not a hair of your head will perish.
In your endurance you will gain your souls.

21.16–19

DESOLATION OF THE SIEGE OF YERUSHALAYIM

When you see Yerushalayim encircled
By armies, then know that its devastation is near.
Then those in Yehuda must flee to the mountains
And those in the city must escape
And those in the fields not go into her,

For these are days of vengeance to fulfill
All that has been written by the prophets:
A plague on those women who have a child
In their womb and women who are nursing
In those days. There will be great distress
On the earth and anger against the people.
And they will fall to the edge of the sword
And they will be taken away as captives
Into all nations, and Yerushalayim
Will be trampled by foreigners[22] until the time
Of the foreigners has run its course.

21.20–24

Cosmic Disasters and Coming of the Earthly Son

There will be signs in sun and moon and stars,
And on the earth the dismay of foreign nations
In bewilderment at the sound of the sea
And surf. People will faint from fear
And foreboding of what is coming upon the world,
For the powers of heaven will be shaken.
And then they will see the earthly son coming
On a cloud with power and enormous glory.
When these things happen, stand up straight
And raise your heads, for your redemption is near.

21.25–28

22 Romans.

PARABLE OF THE BUDDING FIG TREE

Look at the fig tree and all the trees.
When they sprout leaves, you look at them
And know that summer is already near.
So too when you see these things happening
You know the kingdom of God is near.
I tell you truth. This generation will not
Pass by until all these things take place.
The sky and the earth will pass away
But my words will not pass away.

21.29–33

PREPARING THE PESACH MEAL WITH HIS STUDENTS

Look, as you go into the city,
A man carrying a jar of water will meet you.
Follow him into the house he enters
And say to the owner of the house,
"The rabbi says to you, 'Where is the guest room
Where I am to eat the Pesach meal
With my students?' " And he will show you
A large upstairs room, already furnished.
Prepare it there.

22.10–12

THE SEDER[23]

I greatly desired to eat this Pesach with you
Before I suffer.
I tell you truth,
I will not eat it again until it is fulfilled
In the kingdom of God.

22.15–16

TAKE THIS CUP FROM ME

Take this cup from me and share it among you.
I say to you,
As of now I will not drink of the fruit
Of the vine
Until the kingdom of God comes.

22.17–18

BREAKING THE MATZOT BREAD

This is my body,
Which is given for you.

Do this in remembrance of me.[24]

22.19

23 The Last Supper.
24 The ceremony of the thanksgiving, known as the Eucharist, from the Greek for
"giving thanks" [to God].

AFTER SUPPER HE DOES THE SAME WITH THE CUP

This cup is the new covenant in my blood,
Which is poured out for you.

22.20

FORETELLING THE HAND OF THE BETRAYER

But look, the hand of the betrayer is with me
On the table.
Because the earthly son is going away
As has been determined,
But a plague on that man who betrayed him.

22.21–22

AFTER A QUARREL AMONG HIS STUDENTS ABOUT WHO IS THE GREATEST

The kings of nations lord it over them
And those in power are called benefactors,
But with you it is not so,
Let the greatest among you be the youngest
And the leader the one who serves.
Who is greater?
The one who reclines at the table
Or the one serving?
I am among you as one who serves.

22.25–27

You Will Eat and Drink at My Table in My Kingdom

You are the ones who have stood by me
In my trials. And just as my father
Has conferred a kingdom on me, I confer on you
That you may eat and drink at my table
In my kingdom, and you will sit on thrones
And judge the twelve tribes of Yisrael.

22.28–30

Shimon Kefa, Will You Deny Me?

Shimon, Shimon, look, Satan has demanded
To sift you like wheat,
But I have prayed that your faith not fail you,
And when you return you strengthen your brothers.

22.31–32

To Shimon Kefa Who Says He Is Ready to Go to Prison and to Die for Him

I tell you, Shimon Kefa, the cock will not crow today
Until you have three times denied knowing me.

22.34

Now Go Out with a Purse, Bag, and Sandals and Buy a Sword

But now let the one who has a purse
Let him take it, and also the bag,
And the one who has no sword,
Let him sell his coat and buy one.
For I tell you, what Yeshayahu[25] wrote
Must be fulfilled in me.
"Even he was counted among the lawless."
And what is said about me will find resolution.

22.36–37

On His Knees, Praying on the Mountain of Olives

Father, if you choose, take this cup from me,
And let not my will but yours be done.

22.42

To His Students Sleeping after Their Grief

Why are you sleeping? Get up and pray
That you may not enter the time of trial.

22.46

25 Isa. 5.12.

His Student Yehuda, Leading a Crowd, Comes Up to Kiss Him

Yehuda, are you betraying the earthly son with a kiss?

22.48

The Mob Attacking Him

Did you come out with swords and clubs
As if I were a robber?
Each day I was with you in the Temple
You did not lay your hands on me.
But this is your hour, and the power of darkness.

22.52–53

The Sanhedrin Ask Him if He Is the Mashiah

If I tell you, you will not believe me,
And if I question you, you will not answer.
But from now on the earthly son
Will be sitting at the right hand of the power of God.

22.67–69

The Sanhedrin Ask Him, "Are You the Son of God?"

You say that I am.

22.70

BEFORE PILATUS[26] WHO ASKS, "ARE YOU THE KING OF THE JEWS?"

You say it.

23.3

ON GOLGOTHA, PLACE OF THE SKULL, YESHUA AND THE TWO CRIMINALS

Father, forgive them.
They do not know what they are doing.

23.34

TO ONE OF THE CRIMINALS WHO ASKS TO BE REMEMBERED

Today you will be with me in paradise.

23.43

DARKNESS AT NOON

Father, into your hands I commend my spirit.

23.46

26 Pilate.

ON THE ROAD TO EMMAOUS, A VILLAGE SEVEN MILES FROM YERUSHALAYIM, THE RISEN YESHUA SEES TWO STUDENTS WHO DO NOT RECOGNIZE HIM

What are these words you are exchanging
With each other as you walk along?
O what fools and slow of heart you are to believe
All that the prophets spoke!
Did not the mashiah have to suffer this
And enter into his glory?

24.17, 25–26

BACK IN YERUSHALAYIM YESHUA STANDS IN THEIR MIDST

Peace be with you.
24.36

THE STUDENTS ARE STARTLED AND FULL OF FEAR, LOOKING AT HIM AS AT A GHOST

Why are you shaken and why do doubts rise
In your hearts?
Look at my hands and my feet
And see I am myself.
Touch me and see,
Because a ghost does not have flesh and bones
Which as you see I have.

24.38–39

AFTER SHOWING HIS HANDS AND FEET YESHUA ASKS

Do you have something to eat?

24.41

AFTER EATING BROILED FISH

These are my words which I spoke to you
While I was still with you:
All that was written about me in the law of Moshe
And the prophets and Psalms must be fulfilled.

24.44

YESHUA CITES TORAH, TELLING HIS STUDENTS THEIR MISSION TO CARRY THE WORD

It is written that the mashiah is to suffer and to rise
From the dead on the third day,
And in his name you will preach repentance
And forgiveness of sins to all nations,
Beginning with Yerushalayim.
You are the witnesses.
And look, I am sending the promise of my father
To you.
So stay in the city
Until you are clothed with power from on high.

24.45–49

JOHN
(Yohanan)

THE GOSPEL OF JOHN is unparalleled in the Bible. The prologue is magical for believers or nonbelievers, a singular moment in religious scripture and world literature. In theme and structure, the Gospel of John is remarkably independent of the three preceding synoptic gospels. Mark is a poignant and dramatic story. Matthew is a story infused with the lyrics of the Sermon on the Mount and the Beatitudes. Luke adds the nativity tale and long parables, and sings the poor. By contrast, John has less tale than Mark, less of the lyric splendor coloring Matthew and Luke. While it too narrates the life and death of Jesus and includes some beautiful wisdom verse, it surprises with Jesus's brief and long meditations on light, death, and eternity. The voice in the Gospel of John is uniformly spiritual and philosophical.

The creation prologue, beginning with paradoxes of light and darkness, heaven and earth, truth and lies, recalls the dichotomies found in the Dead Sea Scrolls of the Essene community. Amid the eloquent passages of spiritual inquiry in John, there is also a Gnostic element with respect to knowledge and inner light. As a mirror to a time of diverse beliefs and philosophies, John emerges as the gospel of being.

The first luminous lines of John are not lines of poetry spoken by Jesus, but a poetic account of Jesus's voyage to the earth. Like the first lines of Genesis, they say how the world was made through the word and the light.

IN THE BEGINNING WAS THE WORD

In the beginning was the word[1]
And the word was with God,
And the word was God.
He was in the beginning with God.
All things were born through him,
And without him nothing was born.
In him was life
And in life was the light in all people
And light glows in the darkness
And darkness could not cast it down.

1.1–5

As the beginning of Genesis, the beginning of John is a creation story of the world through the word and the light. Here the word means God, the light, and the word that becomes flesh. The essential diction and imagery we encounter throughout the Gospel of John appears in the prologue:

LIGHT WAS IN THE WORLD

The true light glowing in all people
Came into the world.

---

1 John informs us "In the beginning was the word," Εν ἀρχή ἦν ὁ λόγος (En arhe en ho logos) (John 1.1). God created through the word, ὁ λόγος. With that utterance God translates divine sound into matter and being, thereby bringing the cosmos, the earth, and the earth's inhabitants, great and small, into temporal existence. The creation through the word in John parallels the creation in Genesis 1.1 of the Hebrew Bible: "In the beginning when God created the heavens and the earth": בְּרֵאשִׁית בָּרָא אֱלֹהִים אֵת הַשָּׁמַיִם וְאֵת הָאָרֶץ. In Hebrew: bereshit bara elohim et ha-shamayim veet ha-aretz).

He was in the world
And through him the world was born,
And the world did not know him.[2]
He went to his own
And his own did not receive him.
To all who received him,
Who believed in his name,
He gave power to become the children of God,
Who were born not from blood
Or from the will of the flesh
Or from the will of a man,
But were born from God.
And the word became flesh
And lived among us,
And we gazed on his glory,
The glory of the only son born of the father,
Who is filled with grace and truth.

1.9–14

The two poems cited from the wholly poetic prologue to John are at once logical and resonantly simple. The metaphors and paradoxes are clear and cosmically dramatic. The logic is a unique structure for a great poetic discourse as concise and enlightening as any Socratic or Aristotelian syllogism in which the poem finds a formal antecedent. Combining these qualities of Greek logic and biblical cosmology raises this plain poem to the sublime. In earlier literature its minimalist and precise song recalls the beauty of the biblical Song of Songs and the equipoise of the divine and the earthly in Sappho's poems and fragments.

2 Yeshua the Mashiah.

In the Gospel of John, in the prologue as well as in Jesus's immaculate poetry, we linger at the peak of aesthetic and philosophical speech. As an incarnation of light and word, Jesus speaks his words in verse. The invisible poet emerges unequaled in power and spiritual transcendence.

Under the Fig Tree Natanel[3] Tells Yeshua, "Rabbi, You Are the Son of God!" and Yeshua Responds

Because I told you I saw you under the fig tree,
Do you believe?
You will see even greater things.

You will see the sky open
And angels of God ascending and descending
Upon the earthly son.

1.50–51

At a Wedding in the Galil Miriam[4] Tells Yeshua They Have No Wine and Yeshua Responds with a Plan to Turn Water into Wine

Woman, what is that to me and you?
My hour has not yet come.

Now fill the pots with water,
Pour some of the water out
And take it to the master of the feast.

2.4, 7–8

3 Nathaniel.
4 Mary.

PESACH[5] IN YERUSHALAYIM. DRIVING ANIMALS AND VENDORS WITH A WHIP FROM THE COURTYARD OF HIS TEMPLE, YESHUA TELLS THE DOVE SELLERS

Get these things out of here!
Do not make the house of my father
A house of business!

2.16

SEEING HIMSELF AS THE TEMPLE OF THE BODY

Destroy this Temple
And in three days I shall raise it up.

2.19

HIS PHARISEE FRIEND NAKDEIMON ASKS HOW HE CAN PERFORM MIRACLES

Unless you are born from above
You cannot see the kingdom of God.

Unless you are born from water and the wind of God
You cannot enter the kingdom of God.

What is born from the flesh is flesh,
What is born from the wind is wind.

5 Last Supper.

Do not wonder that I told you
You must be born again from above.

The wind blows where it wants to and you hear its sound
But you cannot know where it comes from and where it goes.

So it is for everyone born from the wind of God.
You are the teacher of Yisrael and do not know this?

We speak of what we know, we testify to what we have seen,
Yet you do not receive our testimony.

If I tell you of earthly things and you do not believe,
How if I tell you of heavenly things will you believe?

And no one has gone up into the sky
Except the one who came down from the sky,

The earthly son.
And as Moshe raised up the snake in the desert,

The earthly son must be raised up
So that all who believe in him will have eternal life.

3.3, 5–8, 10–15

GOD'S ONLY SON

God loved the world so much he gave his only son
So that all who believe in him might not be destroyed
But have eternal life.

God did not send his son into the world to judge the world
But so through him the world might be saved.

One who believes in him is not judged
But one who does not believe is judged already
For not believing in the name of God's only son.

3.16–18

THE LIGHT

And this is the judgment:
Light came into the world
And people loved the darkness rather than the light,
For their works were cunning.
For all who do shoddy things hate the light
And do not come toward the light
So that their works will not be exposed.
But those who do the truth come toward the light
So their works may shine as accomplished through God.

3.19–21

TO A SHOMRONI[6] WOMAN DRAWING WATER FROM A WELL

Give me a drink.

4.7

---

6 Samaritan. The Samaritans were a prominent sect of the Jews in Israel.

The Woman Asks Yeshua How He a Jew Could Give Her a Shomroni a Drink

If you knew the gift of God and who is saying to you,
"Give me a drink,"
You would have asked and he would have given you
Living water.

4.10

The Woman Says He Has No Bucket and Asks if He Is Greater than Yaakov and God Their Father Who Gave Them the Well to Drink and Cattle

Everyone who drinks this water will be thirsty again.
But whoever drinks the water I give them
Will not be thirsty again.
The water I give them will become in them
A fountain of water springing into eternal life.

4.13–14

The Woman Says He Must Be a Prophet and Hears of Worshiping in Jerusalem for Salvation

Believe me, woman, the hour is coming
When not on this mountain
Nor in Yerushalayim will you worship the father.
You worship what you do not know.
We worship what we know
Since salvation is from the Jews.

But the hour is coming and it is now
When the true worshipers will worship the father
In spirit and truth,
For the father seeks such people to worship him.
God is spirit
And those worshiping must worship him
In spirit and truth.

4.21–24

THE WOMAN SAYS SHE KNOWS THAT A MASHIAH IS COMING AND IS CALLED THE ANOINTED

I am he, talking to you.

4.26

ANSWERING THE AMAZED STUDENTS WHO TELL HIM TO EAT

I have a food to eat which you do not know.
My food is to do the will of him
Who sent me and to complete his work.

4.32, 34

GRAIN FOR ETERNAL LIFE

Do you not say, "Four more months and then comes the
    harvest?"
Look, I tell you, lift up your eyes

And you will see the fields are white for harvest.
Already the reaper is taking his wages

And gathering the grain for the eternal life
So sower and reaper alike may be happy.

The words of the proverb are true:
"One sows and another reaps."

I sent you to reap what you did not labor.
Others worked and you entered their work.

4.35–38

HEALING A PRINCE NEAR DEATH IN THE GALIL
THROUGH BELIEF

Unless you see signs
You will not believe.

Go, your son lives.

4.48, 50

HEALING A MAN THIRTY-EIGHT YEARS SICK IN YERUSHALAYIM BY THE SHEEP GATE

Do you want to get well?

Stand,
Take up your bed
And walk.

                    5.6, 8

TO THOSE WHO ARE ANGRY FOR HIS HEALING ON THE SABBATH

My father is still doing his work
And I am doing mine.

The son can do nothing by himself unless he sees
The father doing the same,

For what he does the son does likewise.
The father loves the son and shows him everything

That he is doing,
And he will show him greater works than these

So you will marvel.
Just as the father wakes the dead and gives them life,

So the son gives life to whom he will.
The father judges no one.

He has given all judgment to his son
So all will honor the son as they honor the father.

One who does not honor the son
Does not honor the father who sent him.

5.17, 19–23

Eternal Life

One who hears my word and believes him
Who sent me
Has eternal life and does not come to judgment,
But passes out of death to life.
A time is coming and it is now
When the dead will hear the voice of the son of God

And those who hear will live.
Just as the father has life in himself,
So he has given the son life to have in himself,
And he has given him authority to judge
Because he is the earthly son.

Do not wonder at this,
For the hour is coming when all who are in their graves
Will hear his voice and will come out:
Those who have done good will go to a resurrection of life,
But those who have done evil
Will go to a resurrection of judgment.

I can do nothing from myself.
As I hear I judge and my judgment is just,
Since I do not seek my will but the will of him
Who sent me.

5.24–30

BY LAKE TIBERIUS NEAR WHERE YESHUA WALKED ON THE SEA AFTER FEEDING FIVE THOUSAND MEN WITH BREAD

You look for me not because you saw miracles
But because you ate the loaves and were filled.
Do not work for the food that spoils
But for the food that lasts for eternal life,
Which the earthly son will give you,
Since on him God who is father set the seal.

6.26–27

THE PEOPLE ASK YESHUA TO GIVE THEM BREAD

I am the bread of life.
Who comes to me will not be hungry,
And who believes in me will not be thirsty again.
Yet I said to you,
You have seen me and do not believe.
All that my father gives me will come to me
And anyone who comes to me I will not turn away,
Since I have come down from the sky
Not to do my own will but the will of him who sent me.

And this is the will of him who sent me,
That I should lose nothing of all he gave me
But raise it up on the last day.
This is the will of my father,
That all who see the son and believe in him
May have eternal life,
And I will raise them up on the last day.

One who believes has eternal life.
I am the bread of life.
Your parents ate the manna in the desert and died.
This is the bread that comes from the heavenly sky,
So anyone may eat it and not die.
I am the living bread
Who came down from the sky.
Whoever eats this bread will live forever,
And the bread is my flesh,
Which I will give for the life of the world.

6.35–40, 47–51

YESHUA IN THE SYNAGOGUE AT KFAR NAHUM[7] SAYS HIS FLESH IS THE TRUE MEAT, HIS BLOOD THE TRUE DRINK

Unless you eat the flesh of the earthly son
And drink his blood,
You have no life within you.
The one who eats my flesh and drinks my blood

---

7 Capernaum from "kfar," meaning "village." Hence "village of Nahum" is the meannng of Capernaum.

Has eternal life
And I will raise that person up on the last day,
For my flesh is the true meat and my blood
Is the true drink.

The one who eats my flesh and drinks my blood
Lives in me and I in them.
As the living father sent me and I live
Because of the father,
So the one who eats me will live because of me.
This is the bread that came down from the sky,
Not like what our parents ate and died.
Who eats this bread will live forever.

6.53–58

NOT FLESH BUT BREATH KEEPS US ALIVE

Does this shock you?
What if you see the earthly son ascend to where he was before?
Breath[8] keeps us alive.
The flesh is of no help.
The words I spoke to you are the breath of spirit
And are life.
But some among you do not believe.

6.61–64

---

8 Breath from the Greek (*pneuma*), meaning "breath" and by extension "spirit."

My Teaching Is Not Mine

My teaching is not mine but is his who sent me.
Whoever wants to do the will of God
Will know whether the teaching is from God
Or whether I speak on my own.
The person who speaks only from inside
Seeks a personal glory,
But the person who seeks the glory of God who sent us
Is true and has nothing false inside.
Did Moshe[9] not give you the law?
Yet none of you keeps the law.
Why are you trying to kill me?

7.16–19

Who Am I?

You know me and know where I am from,
And I have not come on my own,
But he is true, the one who sent me,
And you do not know him.
I know him because from him I am
And he sent me.

7.28–29

9 Moses.

LOOK FOR ME, BUT I AM GOING WHERE YOU CANNOT COME

For a little more time I am still with you
And then I go away to the one who sent me.
You will search me out and not find me,
And where I am you will not be able to come.

7.33–34

CELEBRATING THE LAST DAY OF SUKKOTH IN THE TEMPLE, HE CRIES OUT

Let anyone who is thirsty come to me and drink!
For one who believes in me, as it says in the scriptures,
"Rivers out of his belly will flow with living water."[10]

7.37–38

TO A WOMAN ACCUSED OF ADULTERY, YESHUA STOOPS DOWN, WRITES WITH HIS FINGER ON THE GROUND, RISES AND SAYS

The one among you without sin,
Let him first cast a stone at her.

8.7

10 The Scripture is uncertain. Isa. 44.2–4 or Zech. 14.8. Zechariah is read at Sukkoth.

THE WOMAN TELLS YESHUA SHE IS NOT CONDEMNED

Woman, where are they?
Has no one condemned you?

Neither do I condemn you.

8.10–11

LIGHT OF THE WORLD

I am the light of the world.
Whoever follows me will not walk in darkness
But will have the light of life.

8.12

TO THOSE WHO QUESTION HIS VERACITY

Even if I testify about myself, my testimony is true.
I know where I came from and where I am going.
And you do not know where I came from
Or where I am going.
You judge according to the flesh.
I judge no one.
And if I do judge, my judgment is true
Because I am not alone,
But I and the father who sent me.
And in your law it is written in Deuteronomy

That the testimony of two people is true.
I am he who testifies about myself,
And testifying about me is the one who sent me,
My father.

8.14–18

WHERE IS YOUR FATHER?

You know neither me, nor my father.
If you knew me,
You would also know my father.

8.19

I AM NOT OF THIS WORLD

I am going and you will look for me
And you will die in your sins.
Where I am going you cannot come.

You are of things below.
I am of things above.

You are of this world,
I am not of this world.

So I have told you
You will die in your sins.

If you do not believe that I am,
You will die in your sins.

8.21, 23–24

WHO ARE YOU?

I am what from the beginning I told you.
I have much to say and much to judge,
But the one who sent me is true
And what I heard from him I speak in the world.

When you raise up the earthly son,
Then you will know that I am
And from myself I do nothing,
But I speak as my father taught me.
And the one who sent me is with me.
He did not leave me alone,
For what I do pleases him always.

8.25–26, 28–29

TO THOSE IN THE TEMPLE WHO BELIEVE IN HIM

If you remain with my word,
You are truly my students,

And you will know the truth
And the truth will set you free.

8.31–32

BRINGING DAY TO THOSE BORN BLIND

Neither he nor his parents did wrong.
He was born blind so the work of God
Might be revealed in him.
We must do the work of him who sent us
While it is day.
Night is coming when no one can work.
While I am in the world,
I am the light of the world.

9.3–5

HE SPAT ON THE EARTH, MADE MUD WITH SPIT, SMEARED IT ON THE MAN'S EYES, AND HEALED HIM, SAYING

Go wash in the pool of Shiloah.

9.7

TO THE BLINDMAN TO WHOM HE GAVE LIFE

Do you believe in the earthly son?
You have seen him
And he is the one talking with you.

I came into this world for judgment
So those who cannot see may see
And those who see may go blind.

9.35, 37, 39

GOOD SHEPHERD AT THE GATE, WHO LAYS DOWN HIS LIFE FOR THE SHEEP

I am the gate of the sheepfold
Whoever enters the sheepfold not through the gate
But climbs up and goes in another way
Is a thief and a robber,
But whoever enters through the gate
Is the shepherd of the sheep.

The gatekeeper opens to him
And the sheep hear his voice
And he calls his own sheep by name
And he leads them out.

When he has put all his own outside,
He goes in ahead of them and the sheep follow
Because they know his voice.
They will not follow a stranger, but flee from him.
They do not know the voice of strangers.

10.1–5

HE EXPLAINS THE PARABLE OF THE GOOD SHEPHERD

All who came before me are thieves and robbers.
The sheep did not listen to them.
I am the gate.
Whoever enters through me will be saved
And will go in and go out and find pasture.

The thief comes only to steal and kill and destroy.
I came that they may have life, and have abundance.

I am the good shepherd.
The good shepherd lays down his life for the sheep.
The hired man who is not a shepherd
And is not the owner of the sheep
Sees the wolf coming and leaves the sheep and runs,
And the wolf ravages and scatters them
Since he is a hired man
And cares nothing about the sheep.

I am the good shepherd
And I know my own and my own know me
As the father knows me and I know the father.
And I lay down my life for the sheep.
And I have other sheep which are not from this fold.
And I must also bring them in
And they will hear my voice
And there will be one flock and one shepherd.

Therefore my father loves me
Because I lay down my life to receive it again.
No one takes it from me.
But I lay it down of my own accord.
I have the right to lay it down
And I have the power to receive it again.
This command I have received from my father.

10.8–18

HANUKKAH IN YERUSHALAYIM, YESHUA
ANNOUNCES HE IS THE SON OF GOD

I told you and you do not believe
The works I do in my father's name
Are my witness. They speak for me.
But you do not believe because you are not of my sheep.
My sheep hear my voice
And I know them and they follow me.
I give them eternal life
And they will not perish forever
And no one will pluck them out of my hand.
I and the father are one.

10.25–28, 30

YOU BLASPHEME. YOU ARE A MAN AND YOU
SAY YOU ARE GOD

Is it not written in the Psalms,
"I have said that you are gods"?[11]
If God called gods those to whom the word of God came,
And scripture cannot be set aside,
Can you say that I whom the father sanctified
And sent into the world am blaspheming
Because I said, "I am the son of God"?
If I do not do the works of my father,
Do not believe me.
But if I do them, even if you do not believe me,

11 Ps. 82.6.

Believe the works
So you may know and see that the father is in me,
And I am in the father.

10.34–38

THE STUDENTS SAY TO HIM, "RABBI, THE JEWS WERE JUST NOW TRYING TO STONE YOU"[12]

Are there not twelve hours in the day?
Whoever walks around in the day doesn't stumble
Since one sees the light of this world.
Whoever walks around in the night stumbles
Since the light is not in that person.

11.9–10

MARTA[13] WHOSE BROTHER ELAZAR[14] IS DEAD FOUR DAYS IN HIS TOMB

Our friend Elazar has fallen asleep,
But I am going there to awaken him.

---

12 The conjunction of "rabbi" and "the Jews" is an anomaly whose contradiction in identity befuddles its intent of concealing Jesus and family as Jews while making Jews appear abhorrent. This famous and implausible instance of anti-Judaism against Jesus's coreligionists is probably a scribal emendation by a late clerical copyist. If these derogatory words are not later interpolation, it remains unfathomable how Jesus should be heard attacking his fellow Jews, which must include his family, disciples, and all his followers. The poem that immediately follows has nothing to do with the accusation, again reinforcing the probability of later interpolation.

13 Marta or Martha from the Greek *Martha*, from the Aramaic *marta*.

14 Elazar or Eleazar from the Hebrew *Elazar*.

Elazar died and I am happy for you
That I was not there so that you may believe.
But now let us go to him.

Your brother will rise again.

11.11, 14, 23

I AM THE RESURRECTION

I am the resurrection [and the life].[15]
Those who believe in me even if they die
Will live.
And everyone who lives and believes in me
Will not die into eternity.

11.25–26

BEFORE RAISING ELAZAR, YESHUA ASKS MARTA IF SHE BELIEVES AND SHE ANSWERS, "YES, LORD, I BELIEVE YOU ARE THE MASHIAH, THE SON OF GOD, WHO IS COMING INTO THIS WORLD

Do you believe this?
Where have you laid him?

Lift the stone.

---

15 Brackets mean that a word or phrase is not in early text and probably later added by a clerical copyist.

Did I not tell you that if you believed
You would see the glory of God?

Father, I thank you for hearing me,
And I know that you hear me always
But because of the crowd standing here
I spoke so they would believe you sent me.

Elazar, come out!

Unbind him and let him go.

11.26, 33, 39–44

MIRYAM WHO ANOINTS YESHUA'S FEET AND WIPES THEM WITH HER HAIR

Let her be, so she may keep it for the day
Of my burial.

The poor you always have with you,
But me you do not always have.

12.7–8

THE HOUR HAS COME WHEN THE EARTHLY SON IS GLORIFIED

The hour has come when the earthly son is glorified.

Unless a grain of wheat falling into the earth dies,
It remains alone.
But if it dies it brings forth a great harvest.

Whoever loves life will lose it,
And whoever hates life in this world
Will keep it for life everlasting.

Let anyone who serves me, follow me,
And where I am, there also will be my servant.
Whoever serves me, the father will honor.

12.23–26

NOW MY SOUL IS SHAKEN

Now my soul is shaken
And what shall I say?
Father, save me from this hour?
But I came for this hour.
Father, glorify your name.

12.27–28

A VOICE CAME OUT OF THE SKY

Not because of me has this voice come
But because of you.
Now is the judgment of the world,
Now the ruler of this world will be cast out.
And if I am raised above the earth
I shall draw all people to me.

12.30–32

BE CHILDREN OF LIGHT

For a little time longer the light is with you.
Walk about while you have the light
So that the darkness may not overtake you.
If you walk in the darkness
You do not know where you are going.
While you have light, believe in the light
So you may be the children of light.

12.35–36

AFTER HIDING OUT, YESHUA CRIES OUT TO THOSE WHO LOVE HUMAN GLORY MORE THAN THE GLORY OF GOD

Who believes in me does not believe in me
But in the one who sent me.
Who looks at me also looks at him who sent me.
As light into the world I have come

So that who believes in me will not reside in darkness.
And who hears my words and does not keep them
I do not judge
For I have not come to judge the world
But to save the world.

Who rejects me and will not receive my words
Has a judge waiting.
The word I spoke will judge him on the last day.
Because I did not speak from myself
But the one who sent me.
The father has given me his commandment,
What I should say and how I should speak.
And I know his commandment is life everlasting.
So what I say, as the father told me, I say it.

12.44–50

AT THE SUPPER TABLE SHIMON KEFA ASKS YESHUA WHY HE HAS STRIPPED, GIRDED HIS WAIST WITH A TOWEL, AND IS WASHING HIS STUDENTS' FEET

What I do for you, you do not know now,
But these things later you will understand.

Unless I wash you, you have no part of me.
One who has bathed need wash nothing
Except his feet
And he is wholly clean, and you are clean
But not all of you. Not the betrayer.
Not all of you are clean.

13.7–8, 10–11

AFTER WASHING THEIR FEET YESHUA PUTS ON HIS GARMENTS AND RECLINES AT THE TABLE

Do you know what I have done for you?
You call me the rabbi and lord,
And what you say is right, for so I am.
So if I your lord and rabbi washed your feet,
You also ought to wash each other's feet.
For I have given you an example
For you to do as I have done for you.

A slave is not greater than his master,
Nor is the sent one greater than he who sent him.
If you know these things
You are blessed if you do them.

13.12–17

AT THE TABLE, TROUBLED IN HIS SOUL, HE PROPHESIES HIS END

I am not speaking of all of you—
I know whom I chose—
But to fulfill the scripture:
The one who ate my bread
Lifted his heel against me.

I tell you now before it happens
So that when it happens
You will believe that I am I.

The one who accepts the one I send
Also accepts me,
And whoever accepts me
Accepts him who sent me.
Amain, amain, I say to you,
One of you will betray me.

13.18–21

THE BELOVED STUDENT LEANING ON HIS CHEST ASKS YESHUA, WHO IS IT?

It is the one for whom I shall dip the matzot bread
And give it to him.

13.26

AFTER SATAN ENTERS YEHUDA, YESHUA TELLS HIM

Do what you will do quickly.

Buy what we need for the supper
Or give something to the poor.[16]

13.27, 29

16 Lines 2 and 3 are words his students thought he was saying to them.

AFTER YEHUDA GOES INTO THE NIGHT WITH A CRUST OF BREAD, YESHUA SPEAKS OF GOODBYE AND LOVE

Children, I am with you a short while.
You will look for me.
And I tell you as I say to the Jews,
"Where I go you cannot also come."

I give you a new commandment
To love each other.
As I loved you, you also must love each other.
By this everyone will know
You are my students
You are my students if you love each other.

13.33–35

ANSWERING SHIMON KEFA WHO ASKS WHERE HE IS GOING

Where I go
You cannot follow me now,
But you will follow later.

13.36

AFTER SHIMON KEFA SAYS HE WILL LAY DOWN HIS LIFE FOR HIM

You will lay down your life for me?
Amain, amain, I say to you
That the cock will not crow
Before you have disowned me three times.

13.38

I AM THE WAY

Do not let your hearts be shaken.
Believe in God and believe in me.
In my father's house there are many rooms.
If there were not, would I have said to you
That I go to prepare a place for you?

And if I go to prepare a place for you,
I will come again and take you to me
So that where I am you may also be.
And where I go you may know the way.

I am the way and the truth and the life.
No one comes to the father but through me.
If you had known me, you would have also known my father,
And now you know him and have seen him.

14.1–4, 6–7

WHO BELIEVES IN ME

Who believes in me will also do the works I do
And you will do ones greater than these,
Because I am going to the father.
And whatever you ask in my name I will do
So that the father may be glorified in the son.
If you ask for anything in my name,
That I will do.

If you love me, keep my commandments,
And I will ask the father for another comforter[17]
To be with you forever,

The spirit of truth that the world cannot accept
Because it cannot see or know it.
You know it because it dwells with you
And in you will be.

I will not leave you orphans.
I am coming to you.
A little time and the world will not see me,
But you will see me.
Because I live, you also live.
On that day you will know I am in my father,
And you are in me and I am in you.

Who has my commands and keeps them loves me.
You who love me will be loved by my father,
And I will love you and reveal myself to you.

14.12–21

17 The Paraclete, meaning in Greek "the comforter."

I Leave You Peace

Anyone who loves me will keep my word,
And my father will love you
And we will come to you and make our home with you.
Anyone who does not love me
Does not keep the word that you hear.
And what I say is not mine,
But from the father who sent me.
This I have told you while I remain with you
But the comforter, the holy spirit,
Whom the father will send in my name,
Will teach you all things and recall all things
That I have said to you.

I leave you peace. My peace I give to you.
Not as the world gives, I give to you.
Do not be shaken in your heart or frightened.
You heard what I told you.
"I am going away and I am coming to you."
If you loved me you would be happy
That I am going to the father
Since the father is greater than I.

And now I have told you before it occurs
So when it happens you may believe.
I will no longer talk much with you,
For the ruler of the world is coming,
And he owns no part in me.
But so the world knows I love the father,
What the father has commanded me I do.

Rise up. Let us go from here.

14.23–31

I Am the True Vine and My Father Is the Gardener

I am the true vine and my father is the gardener.
Each branch in me bearing no fruit he cuts off,
And each branch bearing fruit he also prunes clean
That it may bear even more fruit.
You are already clean because of the word
I have spoken to you.

Abide in me as I in you.
As the branch cannot bear fruit by itself
Unless it stays on the vine,
You too cannot unless you dwell in me.
I am the vine, you the branches.
You who dwell in me and I in you
Bear much fruit,
And when you are apart from me
You have nothing at all.

Whoever does not remain in me
Is cast away like a branch and dries up,
And these are gathered and thrown into the fire and burned.
If you dwell in me and my words dwell in you,
Ask whatever you wish and it will be given you.
My father is glorified that you may bear much fruit
And be my students.
As the father has loved me I have loved you.
Dwell in my love.
If you keep my commandments
You will stay in my love,
Just as I have kept the father's commandments
And dwell in his love.
These things I have told you so my joy may be in you
And your joy be full.

15.1–11

LOVE EACH OTHER AS I HAVE LOVED YOU

This is my command,
That you love each other as I have loved you.
No one has greater love than this,
Than to lay down one's life for one's friends.
You are my friends if you do what I command you.
No longer will I call you slaves
Because the slave does not know what the master does.
But you I have called friends
Because all things I heard from my father
I have made known to you.

You did not choose me
But I chose you and appointed you to go and bear fruit
And your fruit will last,
And so whatever you ask for in my name he may give you.
These things I command you
So you may love one another.

15.12–17

A WORLD HATING US WITHOUT CAUSE

If the world hates you,
Know that before you it hated me.
If you were from the world
The world would love you as its own.
But I have chosen you out of this world
And because you are not of this world
The world hates you.

Remember the word I said to you:
No slave is greater than his lord.
If they persecuted me, they will persecute you also.
If they kept my word, they will also keep yours.
But all this they will do to you
Because of my name,
Because they do not know the one who sent me.

If I had not come and spoken to them,
They would have no sin,
But now they have no cloak to wrap around their sin.
Who hates me also hates my father.
If I had not done among them things
That no one else has done,
They would have no sin.
But now they have seen and hated both me and my father.
And to fulfill the word written in the Psalms,
"They hated me openly and without cause."[18]

15.18–25

WHEN THE COMFORTER COMES

When the comforter comes,
Whom I will send you from my father,
The breath of truth who comes from the father,
He will testify about me.
You also will be my witness
Since from the beginning you are with me.

15.26–27

18 Ps. 35.19 and 69.4.

I Shall Go Away So the Comforter Will Come

This I have told you so you will not go astray.
They will expel you from the synagogue
And the hour is coming when those who kill you
Will suppose they are serving God.
And they will do this because they know
Neither the father nor me.
But this I have told you so when the hour comes
You will recall that I told you.
I did not tell you at the beginning, since I was with you.
But now I am going to the one who sent me,
And not one of you asks me, "Where are you going?"
But because I have said these things to you,
Sorrow has filled your heart.

I tell you the truth: It is better for you that I go away.
If I do not go, the comforter will not come to you.
But if I go away, I will send him to you.
And when he comes he will expose the world
Concerning wrongdoing and justice and judgment:
Wrongdoing, since they do not believe in me;
Justice because I am going to the father
And you will no more see me.
Judgment because the ruler of this world has been judged.

I still have many things to tell you
But you cannot bear to hear them now.
When the spirit of truth comes
He will be your guide to the whole truth.
For he will not speak from himself but what he hears
And will report to you what is to come.
He will glorify me

Since he will take what is mine and report it to you.
All that the father has is mine,
So I said he will take what is mine and report it to you.
In a little while you will no longer see me
And again in a little while you will see me.

16.1–16

WHEN I RETURN GRIEF WILL TURN INTO JOY

Are you asking each other what I meant by,
"In a little while you will no longer see me
And again in a little while you will see me"?
You will weep and mourn but the world will be joyful.
You will be grieved but your grief will turn to joy.

When a woman gives birth she grieves
Because her hour has come,
But when she has borne her child
She no longer remembers her pain
Because of the joy that a child was born into the world.
So now you are in sorrow, but I will see you again
And your heart will be happy
And your gladness no one will take from you.
And on that day you will ask me nothing.
Whatever you ask the father in my name,
He will give you.
Till now you ask nothing in my name.
Ask and you will receive so your joy may be complete.

These things I have told you in riddles,
But the hour is coming when no longer in riddles
Will I speak to you, but plainly I will declare
Concerning the father.
On that day you will ask in my name.
And I do not say to you I will ask the father on your behalf.
The father loves you because you have loved me
And believed that I have come from God.
I came from the father and have come into the world.
I leave the world again and go to the father.

16.19–28

THROUGH ME HAVE PEACE. I HAVE CONQUERED THE WORLD

Now do you believe?
Look, the hour is coming and it has come
When you will be scattered each on his own
And you will leave me alone.
But I am not alone, because the father is with me.

These things I have said to you
So through me you may have peace.
In the world you have pain. Courage.
I have conquered the world.

16.31–33

YESHUA RAISES HIS EYES TO THE SKY, CONVERSES WITH THE FATHER AND PRAYS FOR HIS STUDENTS

Father, the hour has come.
Glorify your son so that your son may glorify you
As you gave him authority over all flesh[19]
So he may give life everlasting to all you have given him.

And this is the life everlasting
So that they may know you, the only true God on earth
By completing the work you gave me to do.
And now glorify me, father, with yourself,
With the glory I had with you before the world was.

I made your name known to the people
Whom you gave me from the world.
They were yours and you gave them to me
And they have kept your word.
Now they know that all you gave me comes from you.
Because the words you gave me I gave them.
And they accepted them,
And they knew the truth that I came from you
And believed that you sent me.

I ask for their sake.
I am not asking for the sake of the world
But for the ones whom you gave me
Because they are yours.
And all that is mine is yours and yours is mine
And I am glorified in them.

17.1–10

19 Flesh in a larger sense meaning "all the people."

I Am Not in This World

And I am no longer in the world
But they are in the world,

And I am coming to you.
Holy father, keep them in your name,
Which you gave me,
So they may be one as we are one.
When I was with them,
Through your name I kept those whom you gave me.
I guarded them and not one of them was lost
Except the son of perdition
So that the scripture be fulfilled.

17.11–12

I Am Coming to You

Now I am coming to you
And these things I say in the world
So my joy be fulfilled in them.
I gave them your word and the world hated them
Since they are not of the world
As I am not of the world.

17.13–14

SANCTIFY THEM IN THE TRUTH

I do not ask you to take them from the world
But to keep them from the cunning one.[20]
They are not of this world as I am not of this world.
Sanctify them in the truth.
Your word is truth.
As you sent me into the world
So I sent them into the world.
And for them I sanctify myself
So they may also be sanctified in truth.

17.15–19

I DO NOT ASK FOR THEM ALONE

I do not ask for them alone,
But for those believing in me through their word
That we may all be one
As you, father, are in me and I in you;
That the world may believe that you sent me.
The glory you gave me I gave them
So they may be one as we are one.
I in them and you in me
So they may be made perfect as one,
So the world may know that you sent me
And loved them just as you loved me.

20 The devil.

Father, wherever I am I want the ones you gave me
Also to be with me and see my glory,
Which you gave me since you loved me
Before the foundation of the world.
Just father, the world did not know who you were,
But I knew you
And these ones knew that you had sent me.

I made your name known to them
And I shall make it known
So the love you have had for me
May be in them and I in them.

17.20–26

WHERE EVERYTHING IS TO HAPPEN TO HIM

Who are you looking for?
I am he.

Who are you looking for?
I told you that I am he.

If you are looking for me, let these men go.
I have not lost one of those you gave me.

18.4, 6–9

AFTER SHIMON KEFA CUTS OFF THE SLAVE'S EAR

Put your knife back in its sheath.
Shall I not drink the cup the father gave me?

18.11

TO THE HIGH PRIEST QUESTIONING HIM

I have spoken openly to the world.
I always taught in a synagogue and in the Temple
Where all the Jews gather. And in secret
I spoke nothing. Why question me?
Ask those who heard what I said to them.
Look, they know what I said.

18.20–21

A SLAVE BEATS HIM

If I spoke wrong, testify to the wrong.
But if I spoke right, why do you beat me?

18.23

Before Pilatus Who Asks, Are You the King of the Jews?

Are you speaking for yourself
Or did others tell you about me?

My kingdom is not of this world.
If my kingdom were of this world
My servants would have fought to keep me.
But now my kingdom is not here.

You say I am a king.
For this I was born
And for this I came into the world
That I might testify to the truth.
Everyone born of truth hears my voice.

18.34, 36–37

Pilatus Asks, Where Are You From?

You would have no authority over me at all
Were it not given to you from above.
Therefore the one who handed me over to you
Has the greater sin.

19.11

NEAR THE CROSS STOOD HIS MOTHER MIRYAM AND MIRYAM OF MAGDALA

Woman, here is your son.

19.26

TO ONE OF HIS STUDENTS

Here now is your mother.

19.27

HANGING FROM THE SPIKES OF THE CROSS

I am thirsty.

19.28

YESHUA BOWS HIS HEAD, GIVING UP HIS SPIRIT, SAYING

It is ended.

19.30

Near the Empty Tomb Miryam of Magdala Thinks She Sees a Gardener. It Is Yeshua, Who Says

Woman, why are you weeping?
Whom are you looking for?

20.15

Miryam Turns, Crying Out, Rabboni! (My Great Rabbi) and the Risen Yeshua Says

Do not hold on to me
Since I have not yet gone up to the father.
But go to my brothers and tell them:
"I am ascending to my father and your father
And my God and your God."

20.17

Yeshua Appears in the Locked House of His Students

Peace to you.
Peace to you.
As the father sent me, so I send you.

20.19, 21

He Breathes Over Them and Says

Receive the holy spirit.

For any whose sins you forgive,
Their sins are forgiven.
For any whose sins you do not release
They are not released.

20.22–23

After Doubting Toma Says, "Until I See the Mark of the Nails on His Hands and Put My Finger into the Place of the Nails and My Hand into His Side I Shall Not Believe" and Yeshua Says

Peace to you.
Bring your fingers here and see my hands
And bring your hand and put it in my side,
And do not be without faith but of faith.

Do you believe because you have seen me?
Blessed are they who have not seen and believe.

20.26–27, 29

A Supplement[21]

STANDING ON THE SHORE OF LAKE TIBERIUS
WHERE HIS STUDENTS HAVE BEEN FISHING,
YESHUA TELLS THEM

Children, do you have any fish?
Cast the net in the waters to the right side
Of the ship and you will find some.

Now bring some of the fish you caught.
Come have breakfast.

21.5–6, 10, 12

AFTER BREAKFAST YESHUA SAYS TO SHIMON KEFA

Shimon son of Yohanan, do you love me
More than they do?

YESHUA SAID TO HIM

Feed my lambs.

21.15

21 An orphan ending.

YESHUA ASKS SHIMON KEFA A SECOND TIME

Shimon, son of Yohanan, do you love me?

21.16

YESHUA RESPONDS TO SHIMON'S DECLARATION OF LOVE

Tend my sheep.

21.16

FOR A THIRD TIME YESHUA ASKS SHIMON

Do you love me?

TO SHIMON HURT BY THE QUESTIONS, YESHUA SAYS

Graze my sheep.

21.17

FORETELLING SHIMON KEFA'S DEATH

When you were younger,
You fastened your own belt
And walked about where you wished.
But when you grow old
You will stretch out your hands
And another will fasten your belt
And take you where you do not wish to go.[22]

Follow me.

21.18–19

ON SEEING THE UNKNOWN MOST-LOVED STUDENT, SHIMON KEFA ASKS, "WHAT ABOUT HIM?" AND YESHUA SAYS

If I want him to stay until I come again,
What is that to you?[23]

Follow me.

21.22

22 The stretched arms indicate crucifixion.
23 The dismissive phrase addressed to Simon Peter, "What is that to you?" suggesting it is none of Peter's business, is, according to John 21.24, "testified and written by the most-loved student," who is Peter's rival. The passage is sometimes called an "orphan ending" or a "second conclusion," since it is not found in the earliest Greek manuscripts. The putdown of Peter, who had earlier three times denied being connected with Jesus, lends a puzzling ending to the Gospel of John.

THOMAS
(Toma)²⁴

I N 1946 THE DEAD SEA SCROLLS were discovered in caves at Qumran on the northwest shore of the Dead Sea, yielding copies in Hebrew, Aramaic, and Greek of biblical documents as well as key scriptures of the Essenes who lived on that arid plain. The Dead Sea Scrolls shook the religious world. A year earlier in 1945, the Nag Hammadi Library was discovered in a sealed jar buried in a farm in upper Egypt near the town of Nag Hammadi, yielding twelve leather bound papyrus codices containing copies in Coptic of fifty-two mostly Gnostic tractates. These are the Gnostic gospels, of which the most famous is the Gospel of Thomas.

A version of this gospel may have been composed, most likely in Greek, as early as the middle of the first century, and may have been written in Syria, possibly at Edessa (modern Urga), where a memory of Thomas was revered and where his bones were venerated. The gospel today exists in translation from Greek into Coptic (late Egyptian), but at Oxyrhynchus were found fragments in Greek dating from about 200 C.E. The year 340 has been a suggested date for the Coptic version buried at Nag Hammadi for safekeeping from the Christian Orthodox church that in those centuries burned whatever Gnostic scriptures it came upon.

Thomas begins with the hidden sayings that the living Jesus

---

24 The translation of the Gospel of Thomas was done by Willis Barnstone and Marvin Meyer.

spoke and Judas Thomas the twin recorded. Thomas's original Aramaic name, Toma, means twin, as it also does in Syriac and Hebrew. The Gospel of Thomas is a collection of 114 wisdom sayings in the voice of Jesus. It is appropriate to begin with number 1, which sets the tone, but the larger order seems to be arbitrary. The book contains no gospel story of Jesus's life but rather a discourse between himself and his students. The speech has the dialectical flavor of the ancient world.

Wisdom sayings are Yeshua's way. There is a multitude of wisdom sayings from the widely circulating wisdom literature of the Near East and Mediterranean cultures, dating back to the second and third millennia B.C.E. The Jewish Bible is a treasure of verse sayings, from Proverbs and Ecclesiastes to the apocryphal Wisdom of Solomon.

Given that there are no clear existing sources for the Jesus story in the Bible, the existence of Thomas's wisdom sayings, which appear in like form in the gospels, seems a likely source for wisdom sayings in the canonical gospels. Indeed, the 114 sayings in the Gospel of Matthew could have been key to the figure of Jesus that the evangelists fleshed out in their own mythic tale of wonder, proselytizing, miraculous healing, crucifixion, and resurrection.

With its constancy of focus on a knowledge or awareness of the unsayable hidden wisdom that forever swings back and forth in a balance of equal opposites, the Gospel of Thomas shares the Gnostic centering on the pursuit and absorption of relative knowledge. And Yeshua makes it easy yet not too easy. He keeps the attainment of knowledge not finite—there are no finalities in this Yeshua—but a process of attainment, a movement. It is never stasis (standing there) but *exstasis*, moving on, ecstasy. Hence we read in saying 2:

Seek and do not stop seeking until you find.
When you find, you will be troubled.

When you are troubled,
You will marvel and rule over all.

There are two realms in Thomas, the physical and the spiritual. As to personal resurrection, in Thomas's dualistic belief system, the spirit alone, not the body, is saved. And we attain the spiritual through finding the light. Crucially, Elaine Pagels in *Beyond Belief* sees in Thomas the Gnostic notion of Jesus as teacher, who is, rather than the light of the world, one who proclaims a divinity of light within us.

There is light within a person of light
And it shines on the whole world.

(24)

But once we hear that Jesus is not the light, yet wait, he is—listen again to his Whitmanian declaration:

I am the light over all things.
I am all.
From me all things have come
And all things have reached me.
Split a piece of wood.
I am there.
Lift up the stone
And you will find me.

(77)

Saying 77 is so much like the ending of Walt Whitman's "Song of Myself," one must ask, did Thomas crib from Whitman or Whitman rob Thomas? Both poets have come upon universal truths, which are not absolute, and in their energy live on debate, dialectic, and contradiction. Look to the earth, they both say. Thomas says to look under a piece of wood or a stone. Whitman says to look under his boot-sole on the grass. Whitman's memorable ending is,

> I bequeath myself to the dirt to grow from the grass I love,
> If you want me again look for me under your boot-soles . . .
> Failing to fetch me at first keep encouraged,
> Missing me one place search another,
> I stop somewhere waiting for you.
>
> *(Leaves of Grass, 52)*

I see Thomas, like the Pauline Letters, as an early direct or indirect source for the gospels, coming perhaps a decade or two decades before the canonical gospels. Or, as others say, a decade or two after. The debate goes on. Along with Laozi's *Daodejing*, biblical Ecclesiastes and Song of Songs, and Plato's *Phaedrus,* the Gospel of Thomas reaches the summit of wisdom and metaphysical and poetic literature. Bloom says it in appropriate metaphors: "Like William Blake, like Jakob Böhme, this Jesus is looking for a face he had before the world was made."[1] It seems to me incredible that so many would take this wondrous Jesus figure and deposit him as the scribbles and musings of a misguided monk in a Syrian or Alexandrian monastery.[2] This unreformed Yeshua is a drink of fresh water from a brook in a summer meadow or on a hill in Judea. His students look on, wondering before his promises and challenge. Dare they drink too? He is the speaker in a vital, sophisticated original work who

---

1 From Bloom, "A Reading," in Meyer, *The Gospel of Thomas*, p. 136.
2 Harold Bloom in a worldly way links the Thomas Jesus to the great mystical poets, while showing his exasperation with writing him off as a late afterthought by an early church father's ditherings: "Whatever surges beneath the surface of the Gospel of Thomas, it is not a Syrian Christian wisdom teaching of the second century." From "A Reading," in Marvin Meyer, *The Gospel of Thomas*, p. 136.

survives worldly measures and distractions. The knowledge of his
vision of peace and light offers all a living breath now.

The first lines of Thomas invite the reader into an unknown
world of knowledge. No book has ever been composed that offers
these mysterious and salvific words:

> Whoever discovers what these sayings mean
> Will not taste death.

These are the hidden sayings that the living Yeshua spoke and Judas Thomas (Yehuda Toma) the twin recorded.

YESHUA SPEAKS TO HIS STUDENTS

1 Whoever discovers what these sayings mean
Will not taste death.

2 Seek and do not stop seeking until you find.
When you find, you will be troubled.
When you are troubled,
You will marvel and rule over all.

3 If your leaders tell you, "Look, the kingdom is in the sky,"
Then the birds of the sky will precede you.

If they tell you, "It is in the sea,"
Then fish will precede you.

But the kingdom is in you and outside you.

When you know yourself, you will be known
And understand that you are children of the living father.

But if you do not know yourselves
You dwell in poverty and you are poverty.

4 You who are old in days will not hesitate
To ask a child seven days old about
The place of life, and you will live.
Many who are first will be last and be solitary.

5   Know what is in front of your face
    And what is hidden from you will be disclosed.
    There is nothing hidden that will not be revealed.

6   Don't lie and don't do what you hate.
    All things are disclosed before heaven.
    There is nothing hidden that will not be revealed,
    Nothing covered that will remain undisclosed.

7   Blessings on the lion if a man eats it,
    Making the lion human.
    Foul is the human if a lion eats it,
    Making the lion human.

8   A person is like a wise fisherman who casts his net into the
        sea
    And draws it up from the sea full of little fish.
    Among the fish he finds a fine large fish.
    He throws all the little fish back into the sea
    And easily chooses the large fish.
    Whoever has ears to hear should hear.

9   Look, the sower goes out, takes a handful of seeds,
    And scatters them.

    Some fall on the road
    And birds come and peck them up.

    Others fall on rock
    And they do not take root in the soil

And do not produce heads of grain.
Others fall on thorns

And they choke the seeds
And worms devour them.

And others fall on good soil
And it brings forth a good crop,

Yielding sixty per bushel and one hundred twenty
Per bushel.

10 I have thrown fire on the world,
   And look, I am watching till it blazes.

11 This firmament will pass away
   And the one above it will pass away.
   The dead are not alive
   And the living will not die.
   On days when you eat what is dead
   You make the dead live.
   What will you do when you are in the light?
   On the day when you were one you became two.
   When you become two, what will you do?

12 Wherever you are, seek out Yaakov the just.
   For him the sky and earth came into being.

YESHUA TELLS HIS STUDENTS

13 Compare me to something
    And tell me what I am like.
    I am not your rabbi.
    Since you drink you are intoxicated
    From the bubbling spring I tend.[3]

14 If you fast you will bring sin on yourselves,
    And if you pray you will be condemned,

    If you give to charity you will harm your spirits.
    When you go into any region and walk through the
        countryside,

    People receive you, eat what they serve you
    And you heal the sick among them.

    What goes into your mouth will not defile you,
    But what comes out of your mouth defiles.

15 When you see one not born of woman,
    Fall on your faces and worship. He is your father.

16 People may think I have come to impose peace
    On the world.
    They do not know I have come to impose conflicts
    On the earth—fire, sword, war.

---

3 Jesus is the enlightened bartender who serves up wisdom.

There will be five in a house.
There will be three against two and two against three,
Father against son and son against father,
And they will stand alone.

17 I shall give you what no eye has seen,
    What no ear has heard,
    What no hand has touched,
    What has not arisen in the human heart.

YESHUA TO STUDENTS ASKING ABOUT THE END

18 Have you discovered the beginning and now seek the end?
    Where the beginning is the end will be.
    Blessings on you who stand at the beginning.
    You will know the end and not taste death.

19 Blessings on you who came into being
    Before coming into being.

    If you become my students and hear my sayings,
    These stones will serve you.

    There are five trees in paradise for you.
    Summer or winter they do not change

    And their leaves do not fall.
    Whoever knows them will not taste death.

YESHUA DESCRIBES THE KINGDOM OF HEAVEN

20 It is like a mustard seed, tiniest of seeds
But when it falls on prepared soil
It produces a great plant
And becomes a shelter for the birds of heaven.

YESHUA TELLS MIRYAM OF MAGDALA WHAT HIS STUDENTS ARE LIKE

21 They are children living in a field not theirs.
When the owners of the field come, they will say,
"Give our field back to us."
The children take off their clothes in front of them
To give the field back to them.

I tell you, if a house owner knows that a thief
Is on his way,
He will be on guard before the thief arrives
And not let the thief break into the house
Of his estate and steal his possessions.

As for you, be on guard against the world.
Arm yourselves with great strength,
Or the robbers will find a way to reach you.
The trouble you expect will come.

When the crop ripens,
The reaper comes quickly with sickle in hand
And harvests it.
Whoever has ears to hear should hear.

YESHUA TELLS THE STUDENTS HOW WE ENTER HEAVEN

22 Like these nursing babies
 Are those who enter the kingdom.

 When you make the two into one,
 And when you make the inner like the outer
 And the outer like the inner
 And the upper like the lower,
 And when you make man and woman into a single being,
 So that man will not be man nor woman be woman,
 When you make eyes in place of an eye,
 A hand in place of a hand,
 A foot in place of a foot,
 An image in place of an image,
 Then you will enter the kingdom.

23 I shall choose you as one from a thousand
 And as two from ten thousand
 And you will stand as a single one.

24 Whoever has ears should hear.
 There is light within a person of light
 And it shines on the whole world.
 If it does not shine it is darkness.

25 Love your brother like your soul.
 Protect that person like the pupil of your eye.

26 You see the speck in your brother's eye
 But not the log in your own eye.
 When you take the log out of your eye,

You will see clearly to take the speck
Out of your brother's eye.

27 If you do not fast from the world
    You will not find the kingdom.
    If you do not observe the Shabbat as Shabbat,[4]
    You will not see the father.

28 I take my stand in the midst of the world,
    And I appear to them in flesh.

    I find them all drunk
    Yet none of them thirsty.

    My soul aches for the children of the earth
    Because they are blind in their hearts and do not see.

    They came into the world empty
    And seek to depart from the world empty.

    But now they are drunk.
    When they shake off their wine, they will repent.

29 If the flesh came into being because of spirit
    It is a marvel,
    But if spirit came into being because of body
    It is a marvel of marvels.
    Yet I marvel at how this great wealth has come to dwell
    In utter poverty.

4 Sabbath.

30 Where there are three deities,
    They are holy.
    Where there are two or one,
    I am with the one.

31 A prophet is not accepted in his hometown.
    A doctor cannot heal those who know the doctor.

32 A city built on a high hill and fortified can't fall
    Nor can it be hidden.

33 What you will hear in your ear in the other ear
    Proclaim from your rooftops.

    No one lights a lamp and puts it under a basket,
    Nor in a hidden place.
    You put it on a stand
    So that all who come and go will see its light.

34 If one blind leads one blind
    Both of them fall into a hole.

35 You cannot enter the house of the strong
    And take it by force without binding the owner's hands.
    Then you can loot the house.

36 From morning to evening and from evening to morning,
    Do not worry about what you will wear.

YESHUA TELLS HIS STUDENTS HOW THEY WILL BE ABLE TO SEE HIM

37 When you strip naked without shame
   And take your clothes and put them under your feet
   Like small children and trample them,
   Then you will see the child of the living one
   And you will not be afraid.

38 Often you want to hear these sayings
   That I tell you
   And you have no one else from whom to hear them.
   There will be days when you will seek me
   And you will not find me.

39 You should be shrewd as snakes
   And innocent as doves.

40 A grapevine has been planted far from the father.
   Since it is not strong
   It will be pulled up by the root and perish.

41 Whoever has something in hand will be given more
   And whoever has nothing will be deprived
   Of the paltry things possessed.

42 Be wanderers.

43 From what I tell you, you do not know
   Who I am, but you are like the Jews.[5]
   They love the tree but hate the fruit
   Or love the fruit but hate the tree.

44 Whoever blasphemes against the father
   Will be forgiven,
   Whoever blasphemes against the son
   Will be forgiven,
   But whoever blasphemes against the holy spirit
   Will not be forgiven,
   Either on earth or in heaven.

45 Grapes are not harvested from thorn trees
   Nor figs gathered from thistles.
   They yield no fruit.

A good person brings good
Out of the storehouse.

A bad person brings evil things
Out of the corrupt storehouse in the heart
And says evil things.

From the abundance of the heart
Such a person brings out evil.

---

5 The attack on Jews, as the attack on women in the dubious 114, seems out of place. During the time of Jesus there was strong rivalry between the competing sects. Hence, we find the flagrant use of "Jew" negatively in the gospels when all figures— Jesus, his family, his followers, and the earliest saints—are all Jews in the Messianic sect that later will be called "Christian," meaning "a messianic." Whatever the true history of these inflammatory verses, they are regrettable and bizarre.

46 From Adam to the baptizer Yohanan,
Among those born of women,
No one of you is so much greater than Yohanan
That your eyes should not be averted.

But I have said that whoever among you becomes a child
Will know the kingdom
And become greater than Yohanan.

47 One person cannot mount two horses or bend
Two bows,

And a servant cannot serve two masters,
Or the servant will honor one and offend the other.

No one who drinks old wine
Suddenly wants to drink new wine.

New wine is not poured into old wineskins
Or they may break,

And old wine is not poured into a new wineskin
Or it may spoil.

An old patch is not sewn onto a new garment
Or it may tear.

48 If two make peace with each other in one house
They will tell the mountain, "Move,"
And the mountain will move.

49 You are lucky who are alone and chosen,
   For you will find the kingdom.
   You have come from it and will return there again.

50 If they say to you, "Where have you come from?"
   Say, "We have come from the light,

   From the place where the light came into being by itself,
   Established itself and appeared in their image."

   If they say to you, "Is it you?"
   Say, "We are its children and the chosen of the living father."

   If they ask you, "What evidence is there of your father in
        you?"
   Say to them, "It is motion and rest."

YESHUA TELLS WHEN THE NEW WORLD WILL COME

51 What you look for has come
   But you do not know it.

52 You have disregarded the living one among you
   And have spoken of the dead.

YESHUA TELLS WHETHER CIRCUMCISION IS USEFUL OR NOT

53 If it were useful, fathers would produce their children
Already circumcised from their mothers.
But the true circumcision in spirit
Is altogether valuable.

54 You the poor are lucky
For yours is the kingdom of heaven.

55 Those who do not hate their father and mother
Cannot be my students,
And those who do not hate their brothers and sisters
And bear the cross as I do
Will not be worthy of me.

56 Whoever has come to know the world
Has discovered a carcass,
And of whoever has discovered a carcass,
The world is not worthy.

57 The father's kingdom is like someone with good seed.
His enemy comes at night and sows weeds among the good
seed.

He doesn't let them pull up the weeds
But says to them,

"No, or you may go to pull up the weeds
And pull up the wheat along with them."

On harvest day the weeds will be conspicuous
And will be pulled up and burned.

58 Who is lucky?
Who has worked hard and found life.

59 Look to the living one as long as you live
Or you may die and try to see the living one
And you will not be able to see.

60 He sees a Shomroni carrying a lamb
As he is going to the land of Yehuda.
He carries the lamb around.
He will not eat it while it is alive
But only after he has killed it
And it has become a carcass.
So it is with you. Find a place of rest
Or you may become a carcass and be eaten.

YESHUA TELLS SALOME WHY HE HAS CLIMBED ON HER COUCH, AND EATEN FROM HER TABLE AS IF HE COMES FROM SOMEONE

61 Two will rest on a couch.
One will die, one will live.
I say, if you are whole, you will be filled with light,
but if divided, you will be filled with darkness.

62 I disclose my mysteries to those who are worthy
Of my mysteries.

Do not let your left hand know
What your right hand is doing.

63 There is a rich person enormously wealthy.
He says, "I shall invest my money so I may sow, reap, plant,
And fill my storehouses with produce.
Then I shall lack nothing."
Those were his thoughts in his heart
But that very night he died.
Whoever has ears should hear.

64 A man preparing dinner for guests
Sends his servant to invite them.

The servant goes to the first and says,
"My master invites you."

The reply comes, "Some merchants owe me money.
They are coming tonight.

I must go to give them instructions.
Please excuse me from dinner."

The servant went to another and said,
"My master invites you."

The reply came, "I have bought a house
And I've been called away for a day. I have no time."

The servant went to another and said,
"My master invites you."

The reply came, "My friend is to be married
and I am to arrange the banquet.

I can't come. Please excuse me from dinner."
The servant went to another and said,

"My master invites you."
He said to the servant,

"I have bought an estate and I am going
To collect rent. I can't come. Please excuse me."

The servant returned and said to his master,
"Those you invited to dinner have asked to be excused."

The master said to his servant,
"Go out into the streets and invite

Whoever you find for the dinner.
Landowners and merchants

Will not enter the places of my father."

65   A usurer owns a vineyard and rents it
To farmers to labor in the garden.

From them he will collect its grapes.
He sends his servant for the farmers to give him

The fruit of the vineyard. They seize, beat,
And almost kill his servant, who returns

And tells his master. His master said,
"Perhaps he did not know them." He sends

Another servant, but they also beat him.
Then the master sends his son and says,

"Perhaps they will respect my son."
Since the farmers know the son is heir

Of the vineyard, they seize and kill him.
Whoever has ears should hear.

66 Show me the stone the builders rejected.
That is the cornerstone.

67 One who knows all but has nothing in his soul
Has nothing at all.

68 Blessings on you when you are hated and persecuted,
And no place will be found,
Wherever you are persecuted.

69 You who have been persecuted in your heart are lucky.
Only you truly know the father.
You who are hungry are lucky
When some other hungry stomach might be filled.

70 If you reveal what is in you, what you have will save you.
If you have nothing in you
What you don't have in you will kill you.

71 I shall destroy this house
   And no one will be able to rebuild.

Yeshua Tells a Man Who Asked Him to Tell His Brothers to Share Their Possessions with Him

72 Who made me a divider?
   I'm not a divider, am I?

73 The harvest is large but the workers few.
   Implore the master to send workers to the harvest.

75[6] There are many standing at the door
   But those who are alone will enter the wedding chamber.

76 The father's kingdom is like a merchant
   Who owns a supply of merchandise and finds a pearl.

   The merchant is prudent.
   He sells his goods and buys the single pearl for himself.

   So with you. Seek treasure that is unfailing and enduring,
   Where no moth comes to devour and no worm destroys.

77 I am the light over all things.
   I am all.
   From me all things have come

---

6 74 is omitted because it does not contain Jesus's words.

And all things have reached me.
Split a piece of wood.
I am there. *
Lift up the stone
And you will find me there.

78 Why have you come out to the countryside?
To see a reed shaken by the wind?
Or see a someone dressed in soft clothes
Like your rulers and your men of power?
They are dressed in soft clothes

And cannot understand truth.

To a Woman Who Blesses the Womb that Bore Him and the Breasts that Fed Him

79 Blessings on those who have heard the father's word
And have truly kept it.
A day will come when you will say,
"Blessings on the womb that has not conceived
And the breasts that have not given milk."

80 Whoever has come to know the world
Has discovered the body
And of whoever has discovered the body
The world is not worthy.

81 Let a rich man rule,
And a powerful man renounce.

82 Whoever is near me is near fire,
   Whoever is far from me is far from the kingdom.

83 You see images,
   But the light in them is hidden in the image
   Of the father's light.
   He will be disclosed
   But his image hidden by his light.

84 When you see your likeness you are happy.
   But when you see your images that came into being
   Before you
   And that neither die nor become visible,
   How you will suffer!

85 Adam came from great power and great wealth
   But was not worthy of you.
   Had he been worthy, he would not have tasted death.

86 Foxes have dens and birds nests
   But the child has no place to lay his head and rest.

87 How miserable is the body that depends on a body
   And how miserable the soul that depends on both.

88 The messengers and the prophets will come to you
   And give you what is yours.
   You give them what you have and wonder,
   "When will they come and take what is theirs?"

89 Why do you wash the outside of the cup?
   Don't you know that he who made the inside
   Also made the outside?

90 Come to me.
My yoke is easy and my mastery gentle
And you will find rest.

He Tells Those Who Ask How They May Believe in Him

91 You examine the face of heaven and earth
But you have not come to know the one before you
Nor know how to see the now.

92 Seek and you will find.
In the past I did not tell you what you asked.
Now I am willing to tell
but you do not seek.

93 Do not give what is holy to dogs.
They might throw them on manure.

Do not throw pearls to swine.
They can turn them into mud.

94 Seek and you will find.
Knock and the door will open.

95 If you have money, do not lend it at interest,
But give to someone
From whom you will not get it back.

96 The father's kingdom is like a woman
Who took a little yeast, hid it in dough,

And made large loaves of bread.
Whoever has ears should hear.

97 The father's kingdom is like a woman
Who is carrying a jar full of meal.
While she is walking along a distant road
The handle of the jar breaks
And the meal spills behind her along the road.
She doesn't know it.
She notices no problem.
When she reaches her house she puts the jar down
And finds it empty.

98 The father's kingdom is like a man
Who wants to put someone powerful to death.
At home he draws his sword
And thrusts it into the wall
To find out whether his hand goes in.
Then he kills the powerful man.

YESHUA TELLS HIS STUDENTS ABOUT HIS BROTHERS AND MOTHER STANDING OUTSIDE

99 Those here who do the will of my father
Are my brothers and my mother.
They will enter my father's kingdom.

100 Give Caesar the things that are Caesar's,
Give God the things that are God's,
And give me what is mine.

101 Whoever does not hate his father and mother
As I do
Cannot be my student.
Whoever does not love their father and mother
As I do
Cannot be my student.
My mother gave me lies,
My true mother gave me life.

102 Shame on the Prushim.
They are like a dog sleeping in the cattle manger.

103 You are lucky if you know where the robbers will enter
So you can wake up, rouse your estate,
And arm yourself before they break in.

TO THOSE WHO ASK YESHUA TO PRAY AND FAST

104 What sin have I committed
Or how have I been undone?

When the bridegroom leaves the wedding chamber,
Then let the people fast and pray.

105 Whoever knows the father and mother
Will be called the child of a whore.

106 When you make two into one,
You will become children.
When you say, "Mountain, *move*,"
The mountain will move.

107 The kingdom is like a shepherd who has a hundred sheep
Hidden in his field.
One of them, the largest, goes astray.
He leaves the ninety-nine and looks for the one until he finds
it.
After so much trouble he says to the sheep,
"I love you more than the ninety-nine."

108 Whoever drinks from my mouth will become like me.
I myself shall become him
And the hidden will be revealed.

109 The kingdom is like a man who has a treasure in his field.
He doesn't know it.
And when he dies he leaves the field to his son.
The son doesn't know.
He takes over the field and sells it.
The buyer is plowing and finds the treasure,
And begins to lend money at interest to whomever he
wishes.

110 You who have found the world
And become rich
Renounce the world.

111 The heavens and earth will roll up before you.
And you who live from the living one will not see death.
Doesn't Yeshua say?
"The world is not worthy of whoever has found himself."

112 Shame on flesh that depends on soul.
Shame on soul that depends on flesh.

TO HIS STUDENTS WHO ASK, WHEN WILL THE
KINGDOM COME?

113 The kingdom of heaven will not come because you are
looking for it.
No one will announce, "Look, it's here,"
Or "Look, it's there."
The father's kingdom is spread out over the earth
And people do not see it.

114 Look, I shall guide Miryam to make her male,
So she too may become a living spirit resembling you.
Every female who becomes male
Will enter the kingdom of heaven.[7]

---

7 The anti-female ending is painful and cannot simply be explained away. It is traditional for the time, alas. However, since all ancient texts survive because they have
been copied and recopied, it is possible, if not probable, that this version of Thomas,
both copied and translated from Greek into Coptic, has been *emended* to include an
anti-feminine ending for the book. What makes an interpolating hand likely is that
the book has emphasized a "salvation now" theme; the kingdom of heaven is right
here on earth, as it says in 113. Suddenly the reference to an afterlife in the verse
"Will enter the kingdom of heaven" seems to resemble the orphan endings of the
canonical gospels: scribal interpolation not found in the earliest texts. Such *interpola-
tions* are clear in Paul's 1 Corinthians 33–35, in which Paul orders women to be silent
in the synagogues and learn only from their husbands at home. This passage stands
alone in Paul, who favored women as his apostles ("deacons," he calls them) to estab-
lish new churches for his fellow messianic Jews. In contrast to common belief, Paul is
probably innocent of charges of being against women. All the letters, including the
Pauline letters, show Paul's trust in women for the hardest tasks of forming new
churches and keeping them in order. His record makes him completely justify, not
oppose, the inclusion of women at every level of an emerging church.

GLOSSARY

Adonai. Lord.
Aharon. Aaron.
Amorah. Gomorrah.
Andreas. Andrew.
Avraham. Abraham.

Baal Zebub. Beelzebub.
Baal Zebul. Beelzebul.

Elazar. Eleazar, Lazarus.
Eliyahu, Eliyah. Elijah, Elias.

Galil. Galilee.
Gat Shmanim. Gethsemane.
Gei Hinnom, Gei Ben Hinnom. Gehenna (hell).
Gulgulta. Golgotha.

Kefa, Shimon Kefa. Cephas (Latinization), Peter, Simon Peter, Simeon
    Peter.
Keriot. Iscariot.
Kfar Nahum, Kefar Nahum. Capernaum.

Levi. Levi, Matthew.
Loukas. Luke.
Loukios. Lucius.

Magdala (town on Sea of Galilee). Mary the Magdalene (from Magdala).

Markos. Mark.

Marta. Martha.

Mashiah. Messiah.

Mattityah. Matthias.

Mattityahu, Mattai. Matthew.

Miryam. Mary.

Moshe, Mosheh. Moses.

Naftali. Naphtali.

Nakdeimon. Nikodemos, Nicodemus.

Natan. Nathan.

Natanel. Nathanael.

Natzeret. Nazareth.

Natzrati. Nazarene.

Parush. Pharisee.

Pesach, Pesah. Passover.

Pilatus. Pilate.

Prushim, Perushim. Pharisees.

Sanhedrin. Council.

Seder. Easter Meal.

Shabbat, Shabat. Sabbath.

Shaul. Saul, Paul.

Shehem. Sychar, Syhem.

Sheol. Hell.

Shet. Seth.

Shiloah. Siloam.

Shimon. Simon, Simeon.

Shimon Kefa. Simon Peter.

Shlomit. Salome.

Shlomoh. Solomon.

Shomron. Samaria.

Shomroni. Samaritan.

Shomronim. Samaritans.

Sukkah, Sukkoth. Sukkot, Tabernacle, Festival of the Booths.

Theofilos. Theophilus.

Toma. Thomas.

Torah. Pentateuch (Five Books of Moses); generally signifies the Old Testament.

Yaakov. Jacob, James.

Yahweh, Yahveh, YHWH. Adonai, God.

Yannai. Jannai.

Yarden. Jordan.

Yehoniah. Jechoniah.

Yehuda. Judas, Juda, Judah, Jude.

Yehuda. Judea.

Yehuda man of Keriot. Judas Iscariot.

Yeriho. Jericho.

Yerushalayim. Jerusalem.

Yeshayahu, Yeshayah. Isaiah.

Yeshua. Joshua, Yehoshua, Jehoshua, Jesus.

Yeshua the Mashiah. Jesus the Christ.

Yeshua ben Yosef (Hebrew). Jesus son of Joseph.

Yirmiyahu, Yirmiyah. Jeremiah.

Yisrael. Israel.

Yohanan. John.

Yona. Jona.

Yonah. Jonah.
Yosef. Joseph.

Zakai. Zacchaeus.
Zavdai. Zebedee.
Zeharyahu, Zharyahu. Zacharias, Zechariah.
Zvulun. Zebulun.

CHAPTER AND VERSE OF POEMS

Gospel of Mark

Gospel of Matthew

Gospel of John

BIBLIOGRAPHY[1]

Aland, Kurt, and Barbara Aland. *United Bible Societies Greek New Testament.* 4th United Bible Societies ed. Stuttgart, Germany: Deutsche Bibelgesellshaft, 1993.

Aland, Kurt, Barbara Aland, and Johannes Karavidopoulos. *Nestle-Aland Novum Testamentum Graece* (Greek ed.) 27th rev. ed. Stuttgart, Germany: Deutsche Bibelgesellschaft, 2006.

Alter, Robert. *The Art of Biblical Poetry.* New York: Basic Books, 1987.

—————. *Genesis: Translation and Commentary.* New York: W. W. Norton, 1996.

—————. *The Book of Psalms: A Translation with Commentary.* New York: W. W. Norton, 2007.

Barnstone, Willis. *The Poems of St. John of the Cross.* New York: New Directions, 1972.

—————. *The Poetics of Translation: History, Theory, Practice.* New Haven: Yale University Press, 1993.

—————. *The Apocalypse.* New York: New Directions, 2000.

—————, ed. *The Other Bible.* San Francisco: Harper and Row, 1984; 2nd rev. ed., San Francisco: HarperSanFrancisco, 2005.

---

[1] For a full bibliographic reference to the New Testament and the history of its translation, see Willis Barnstone, *The Restored New Testament* (New York: W. W. Norton, 2009), pp. 1461-68.

———. *The Complete Poems of Sappho.* Boston: Shambhala Books, 2009.

———. *The Restored New Testament: A New Translation with Commentary, Including the Gnostic Gospels Thomas, Mary, and Judas.* New York, W. W. Norton, 2009.

Barnstone, Willis, and Marvin Meyer, eds. *The Gnostic Bible.* Boston: Shambhala Books, 2003.

Bloom, Harold. "A Reading." In Marvin Meyer, *The Gospel of Thomas: The Hidden Sayings of Jesus.* San Francisco: Harper San Francisco, 1992.

Crossan, John Dominic. *The Essential Jesus: Original Sayings and the Earliest Images.* San Francisco: HarperCollins, 1994.

Hammond, Gerald. *The Making of the English Bible.* New York: Philosophical Library, 1983.

Pagels, Elaine. *The Gnostic Gospels.* New York: Random House, 1979.

Spong, John Shelby. *Liberating the Gospels: Reading the Bible with Jewish Eyes: Freeing Jesus from 2,000 Years of Misunderstanding.* San Francisco: Harper San Francisco, 1996.

Trobisch, David. *The First Edition of the New Testament.* New York: Oxford University Press, 2000.

Tyndale, William. *Tyndale's New Testament.* Trans. William Tyndale. Ed. David Daniell. New Haven: Yale University Press, 1989.

Vermes, Geza. *Jesus the Jew.* Philadelphia: Fortress Press, 1981.

———. *The Complete Dead Sea Scrolls in English.* London: Allen Lane/Penguin Press, 1997.

———. *The Changing Faces of Jesus.* New York: Viking Compass, 2001.

ACKNOWLEDGMENTS

I wish to express warmth to those who have helped me in this unusual venture and eased me from error. Two earlier editors incited this twenty-year mission of bringing the New Testament into English. James Laughlin, founder of New Directions, published my book, *The Poems of Saint John of the Cross*, and subsequently ordered me to write *The Poetics of Translation: History, Theory, and Practice* in which Bible scripture is the main paradigm; the book explores the history of Bible translation. This volume led me to translate the whole New Testament. Declan Spring, a marvelous editor at New Directions, published *Apocalypse* (Revelation), the last visionary book of the New Testament and first New Testament scripture I published. William McCulloh, a professor of classics at Kenyon College and collaborator with me in books of classical Greek poetry, X-rayed *The Restored New Testament* lexically and linguistically for mistakes. From *The Restored New Testament* come all poems of Jesus Christ.

Marvin Meyer, the editor of *The Nag Hammadi Scriptures* and *The Gnostic Bible* and the Griset Professor of Bible and Christian Studies at Chapman University, is a world expert in Coptic language and literatures. We have together translated the Gospel of Thomas for this volume. Marvin is always a call away with erudition and endless friendship. In my family I thank Helle Tzalopoulou Barnstone, who gave me a love for everything Greek and unfailingly led me through the Greek tongues—modern, classical, Byzantine, and

Koine—while spelling correctly in all her languages. My daughter Aliki Barnstone, translator of *The Complete Poems of C. P. Cavafy*, helped me with her poetic intuition and biblical knowledge. My son Tony Barnstone, who suggested this book and its title, went through it with tenacious brilliance. My son Robert Barnstone, architect of the sculptured line, helped me cut my lines clean and constantly kept my spirits high. My wife Sarah Handler profoundly considered all aspects of this book, page by page, bringing her skills as a Chinese art historian into the technical mysteries of Bible scholarship.

At W. W. Norton I am for earthly eternity in debt to my editor Jill Bialosky for making *The Restored New Testament* and *The Poems of Jesus Christ* happen and for guiding their passage to fruition. Her assistant Alison Liss has been cardinal in the day-to-day process of carrying the book to completion. Those who have been extraordinary friends in biblical endeavors are wittily erudite Frederick Crews at the University of California, Berkeley, and four poets. They are Gerald Stern, unique and enormous in the world of the poem, life, and Qoheleth's wisdom sayings in Ecclesiastes; Yusef Komunyakaa, who keeps an enlightened Bible in his blood and pen; esteemed Andrei Codrescu of the *Arabian Nights* who is always there, even when lost in the forests of Arkansas, sharing Bible talk with the postman minister; and Stanley Moss, because he is a poet in the prophetic tradition of informed outrage and mastery who has never ceased to encourage all my mischief. In the end I also thank the indifferent ghost of time, who has let me enjoy years of reading and plotting and held me to the ways of composition and spiritual loneliness.